Mandala Designs Volume II
Advanced Adult Coloring Book

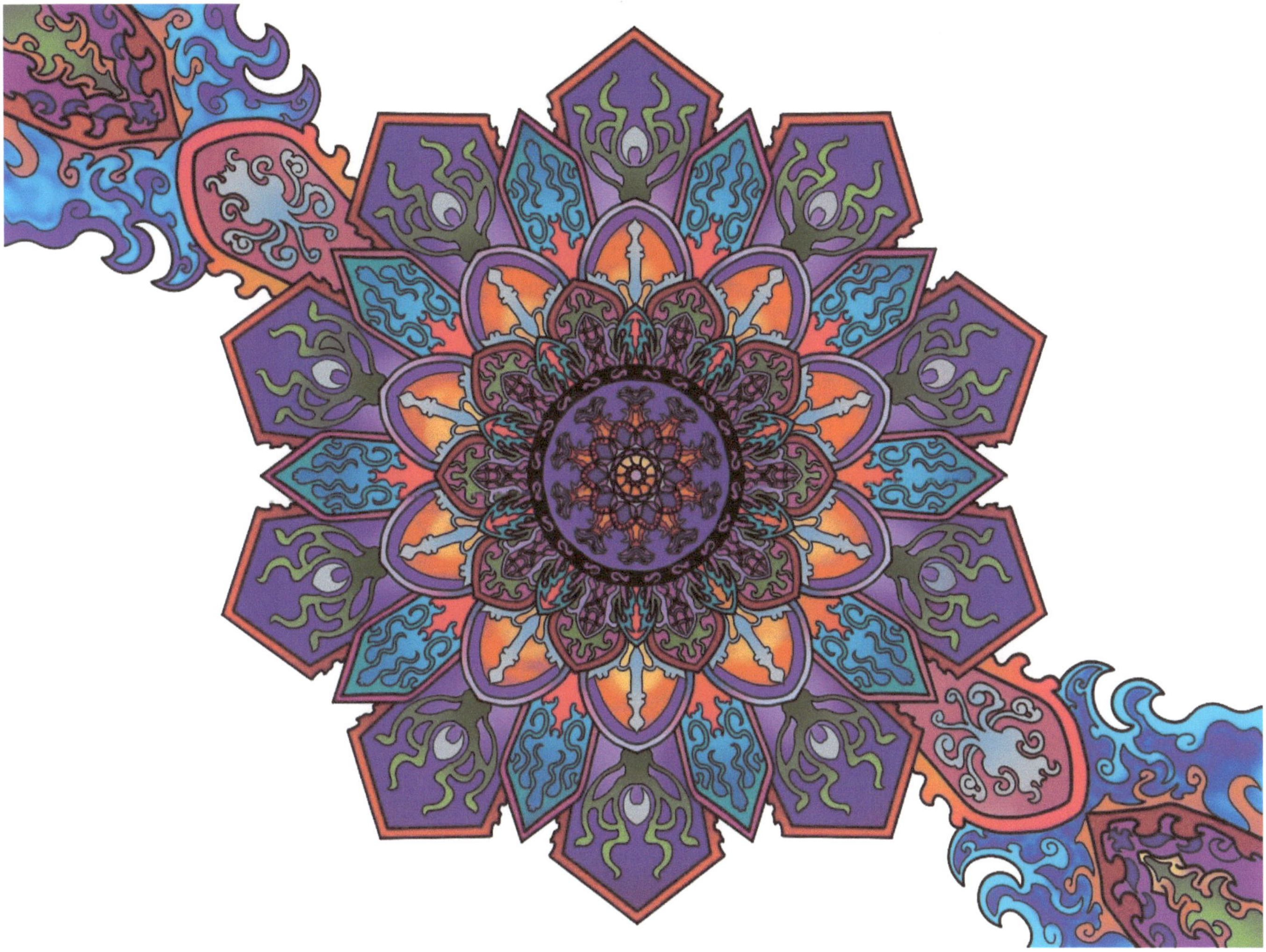

Adrian Sanqui

Mendon Cottage Books

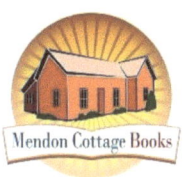

JD-Biz Publishing

Download Free Books!
http://MendonCottageBooks.com

All Rights Reserved.

No part of this publication may be reproduced in any form or by any means, including scanning, photocopying, or otherwise without prior written permission from JD-Biz Corp Copyright © 2018

All Images Licensed by Adrian Sanqui, Fotolia, Pixabay, and 123RF.

Disclaimer

The information is this book is provided for informational purposes only. The information is believed to be accurate as presented based on research by the author.

The author or publisher is not responsible for the use or safety of any procedure or treatment mentioned in this book. The author or publisher is not responsible for errors or omissions that may exist.

Our books are available at

1. Amazon.com
2. Barnes and Noble
3. Itunes
4. Kobo
5. Smashwords
6. Google Play Books

Download Free Books!
http://MendonCottageBooks.com

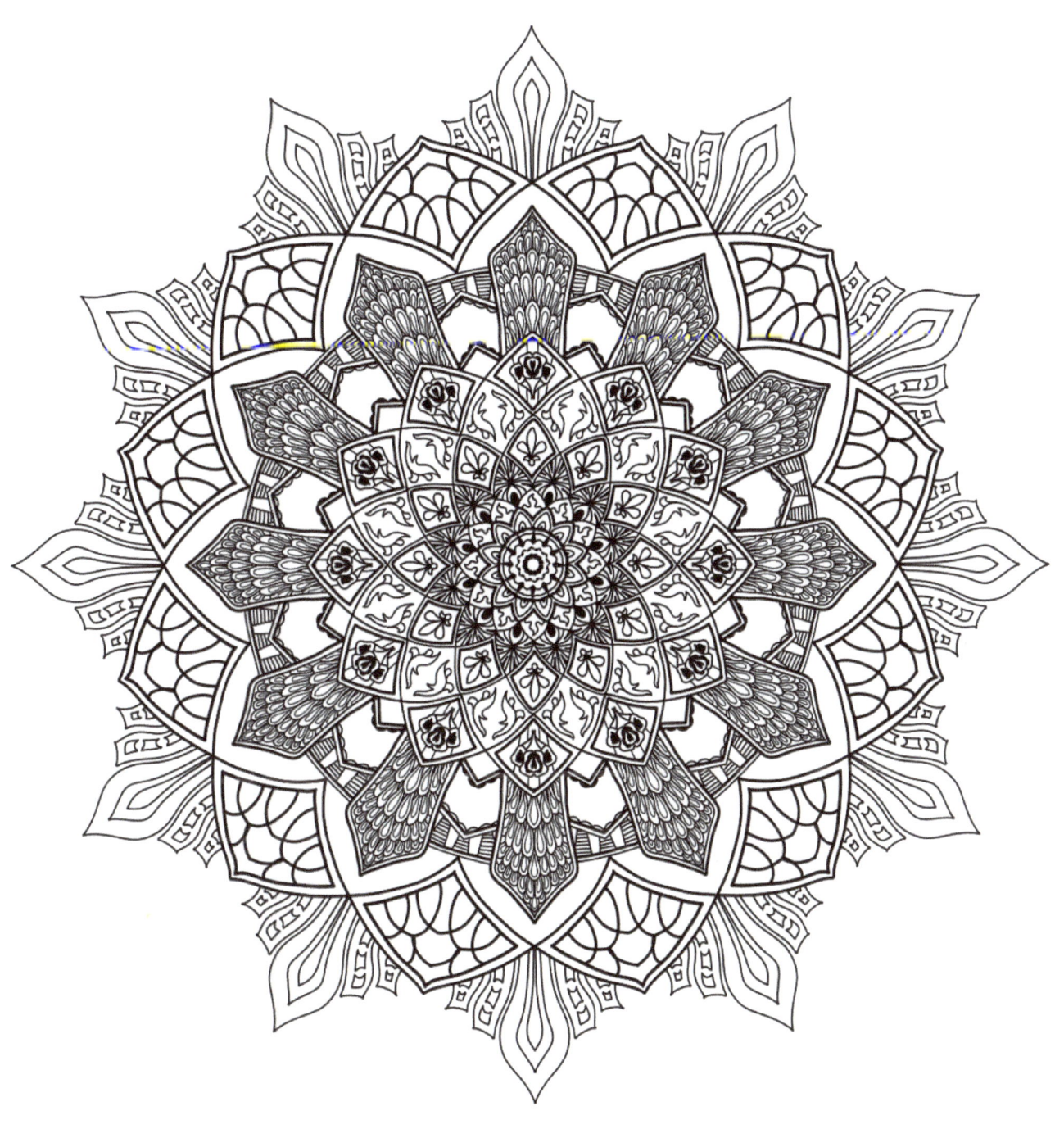

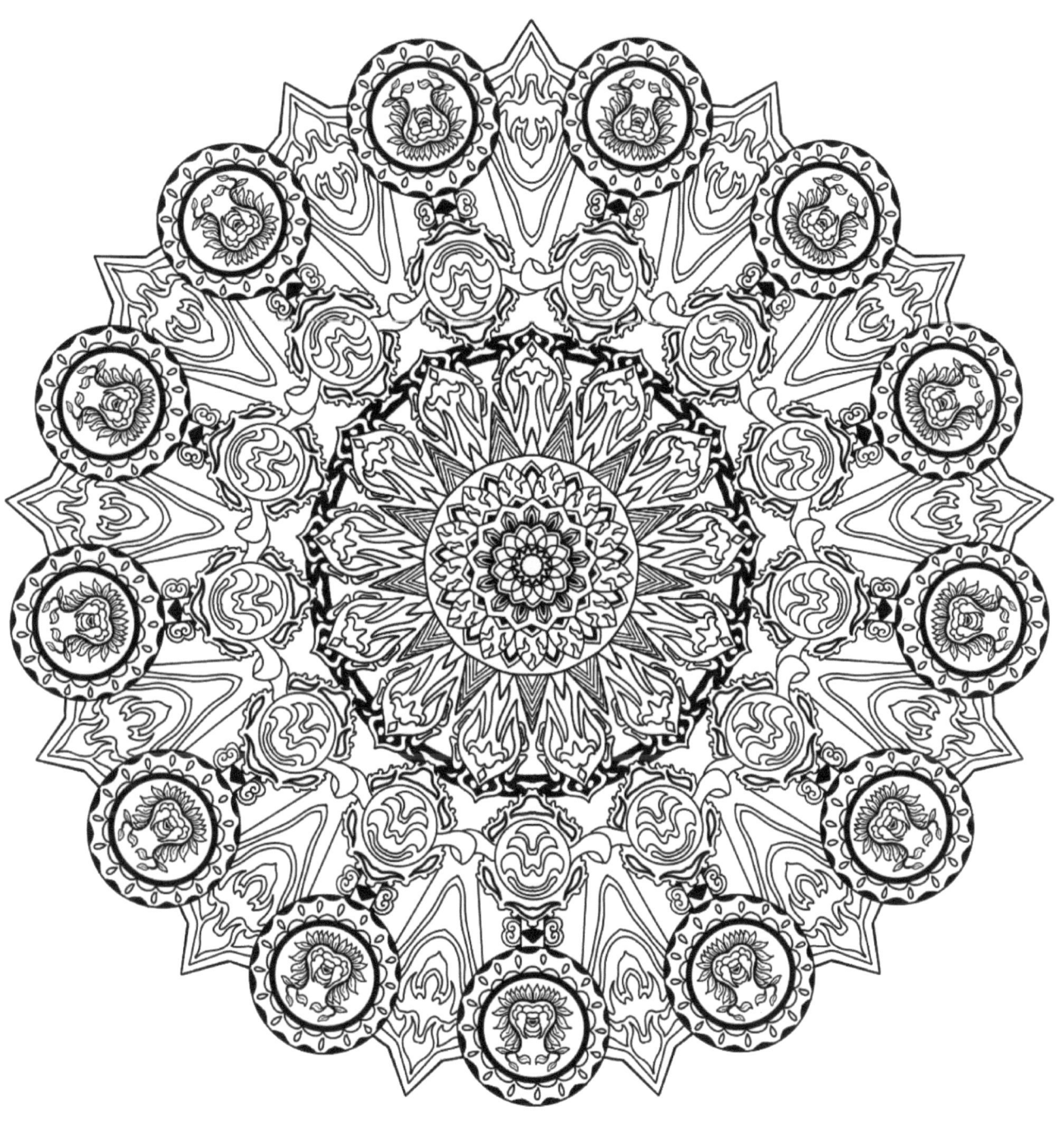

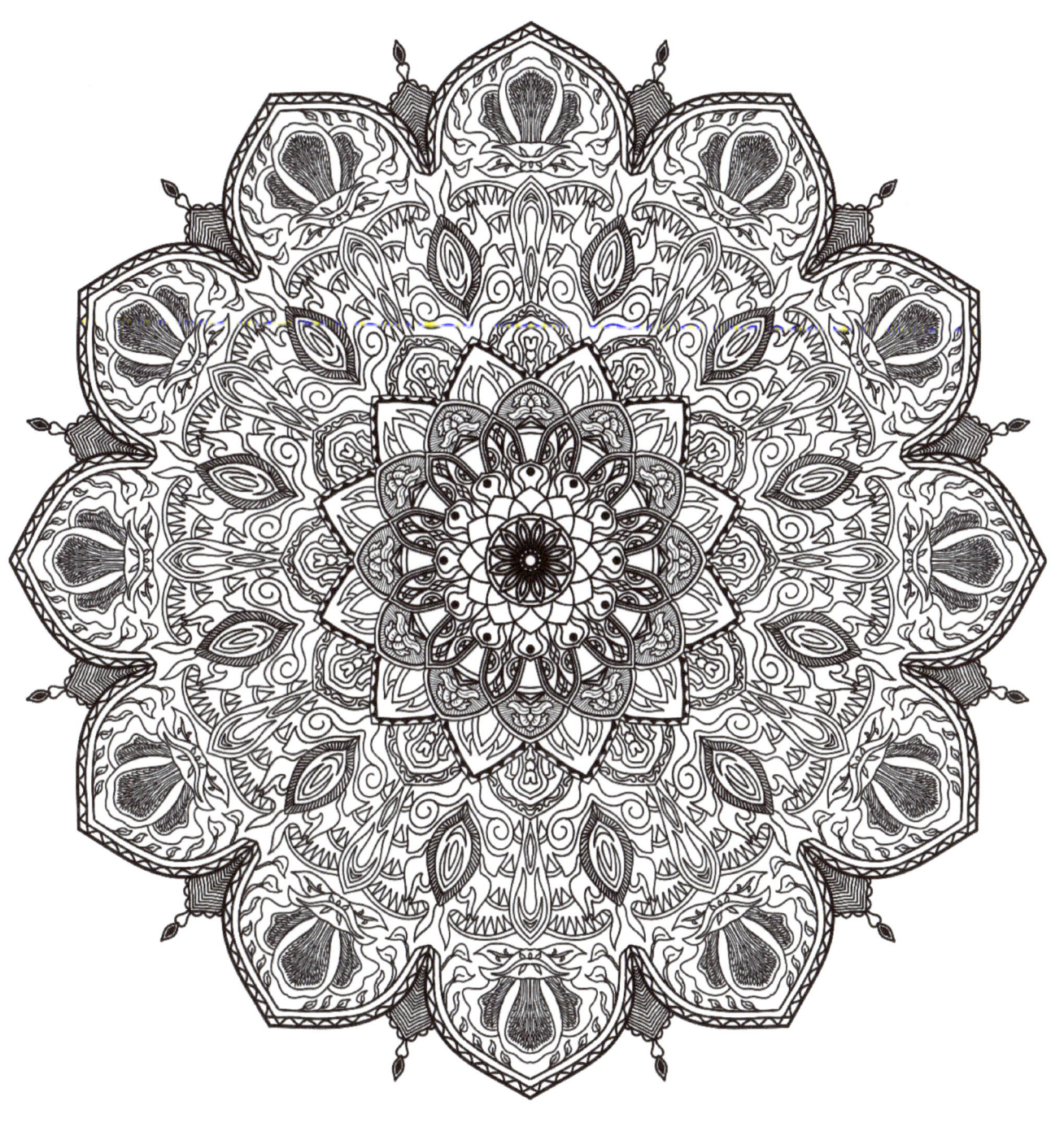

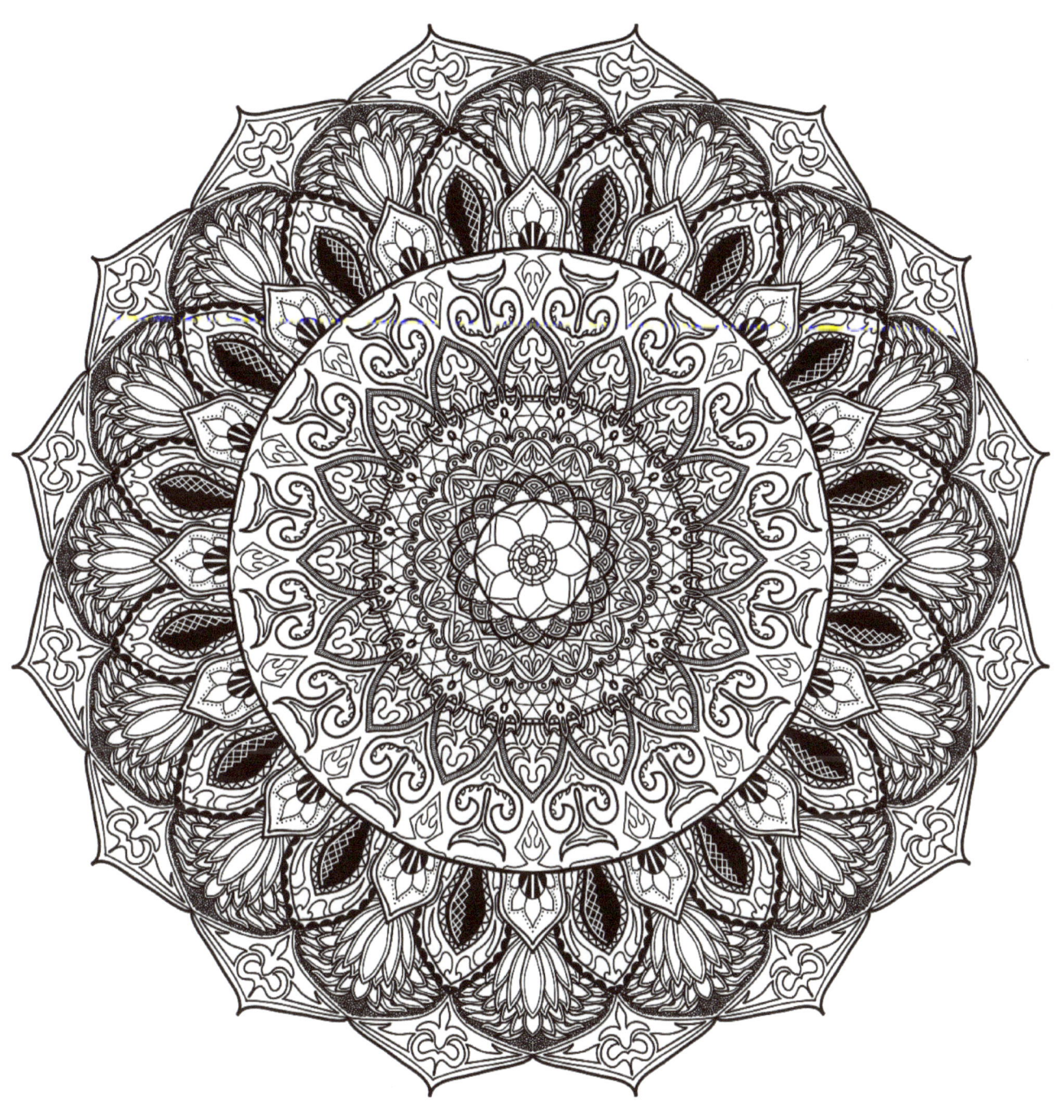

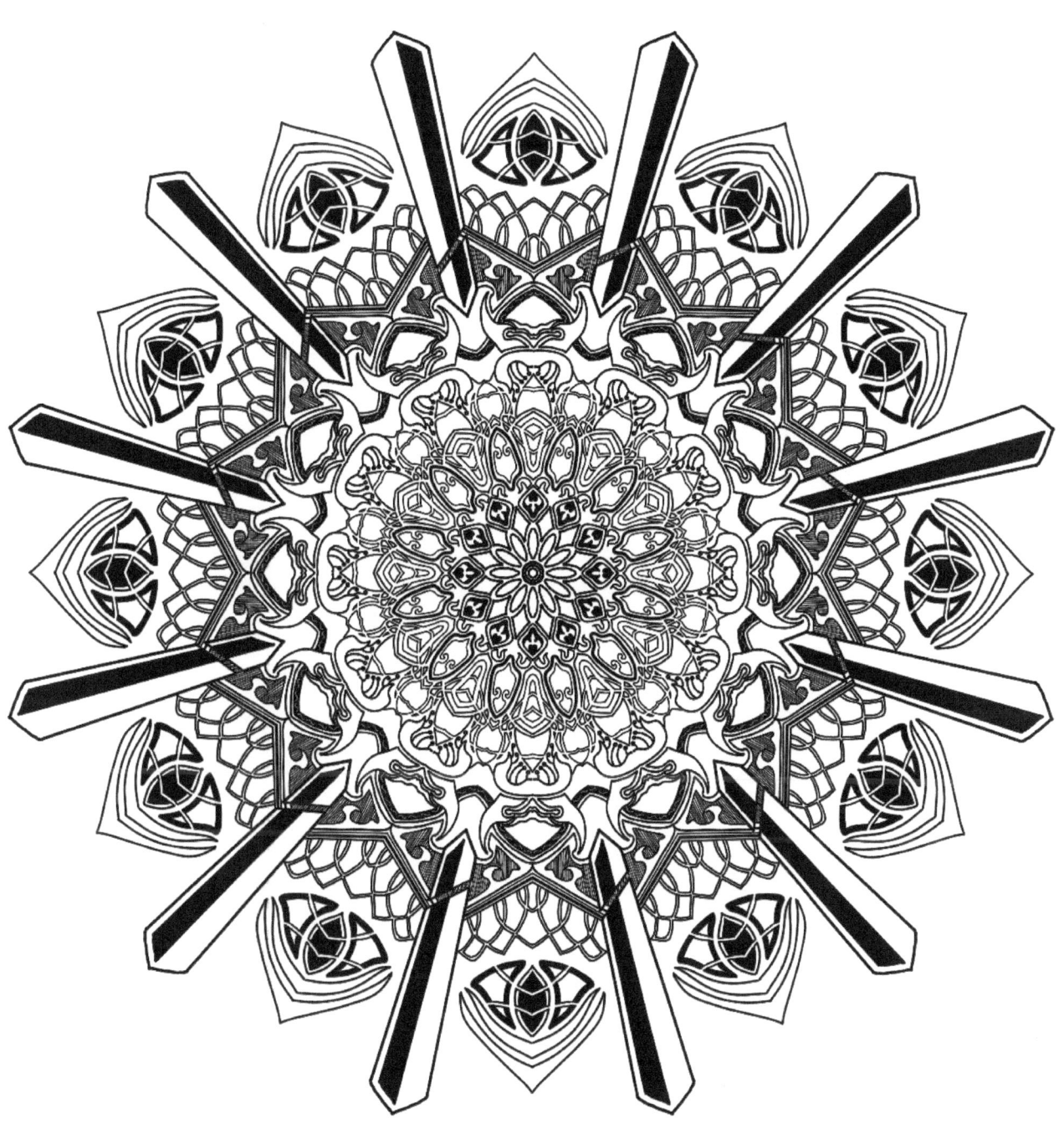

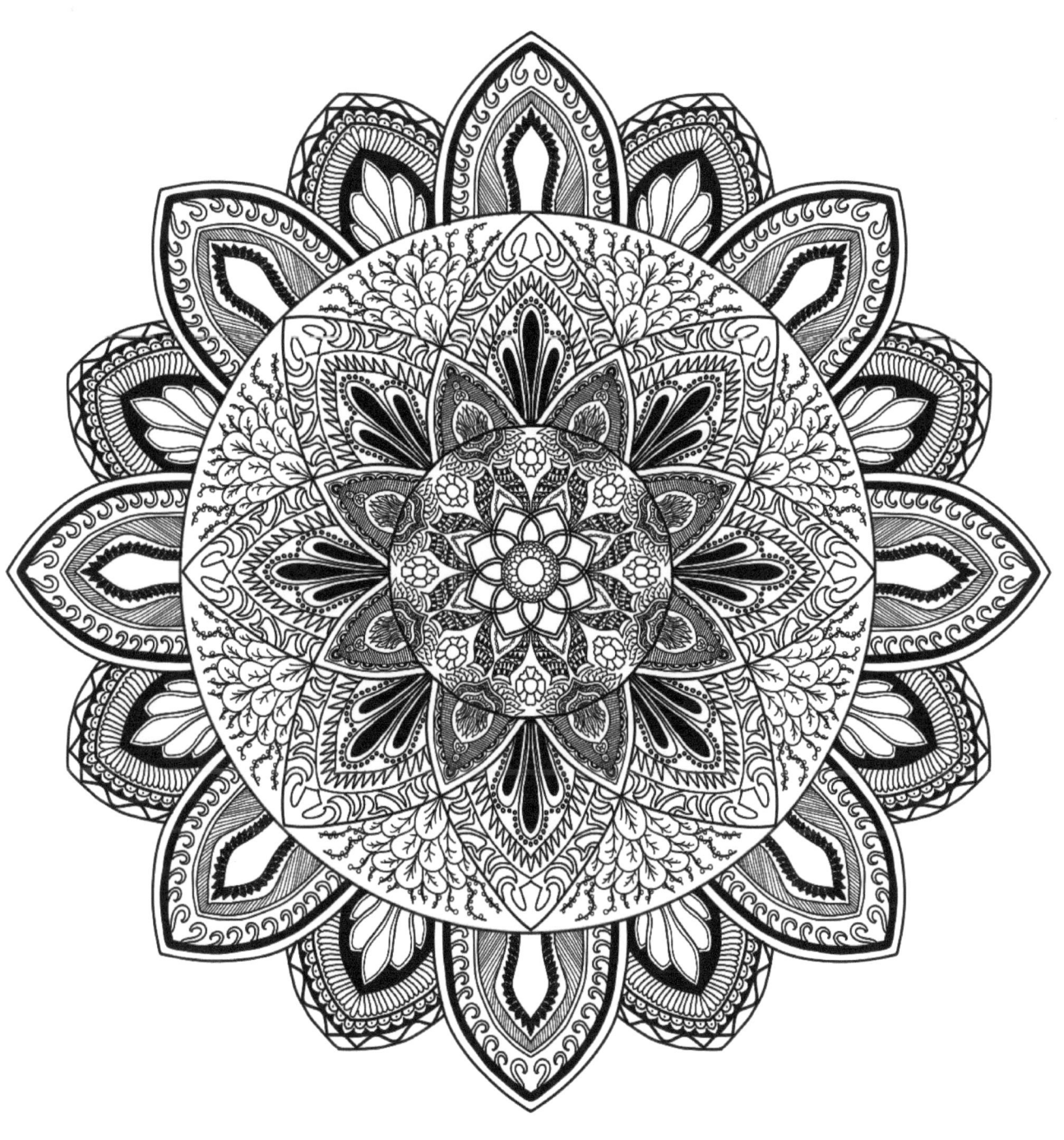

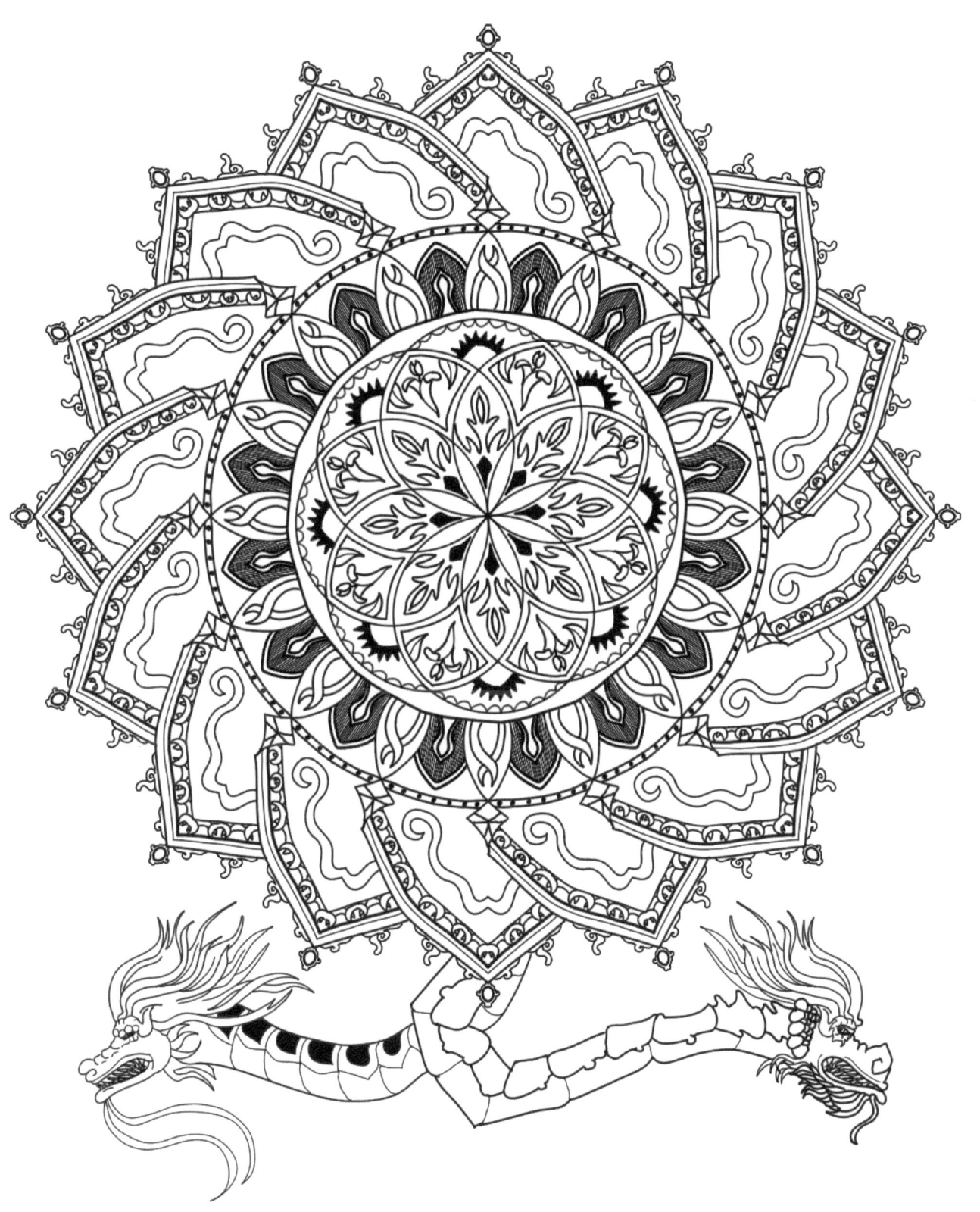

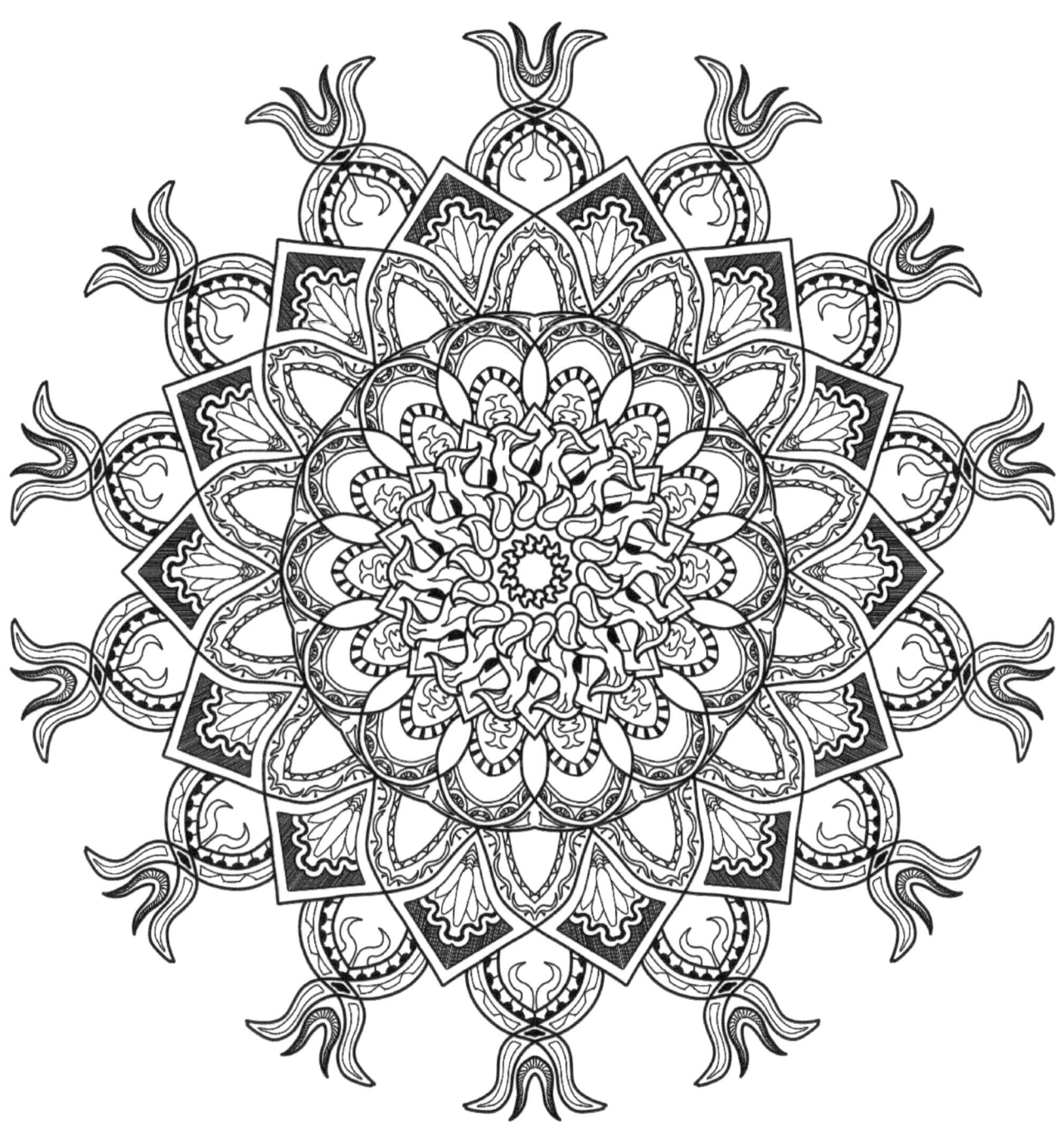

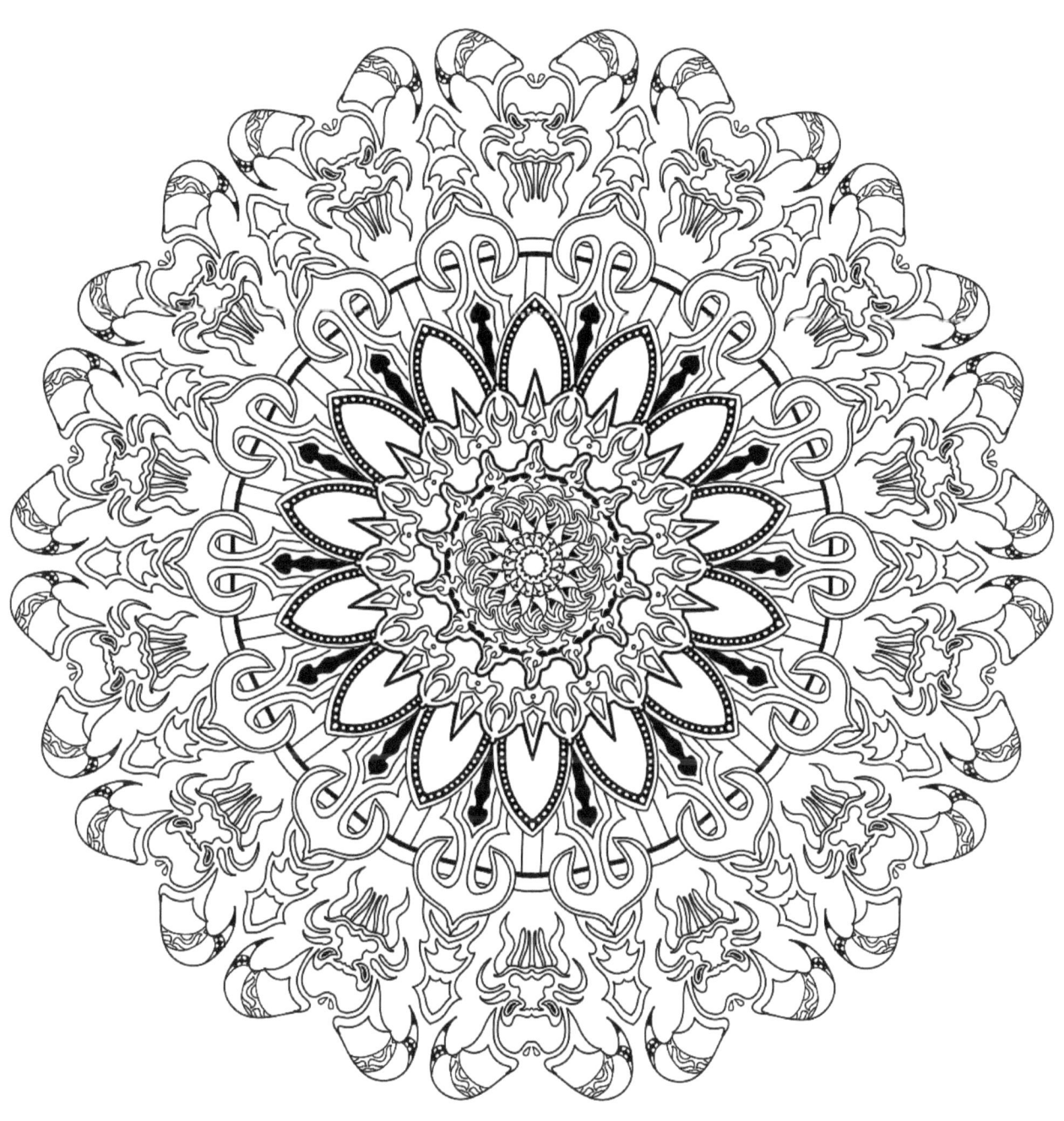

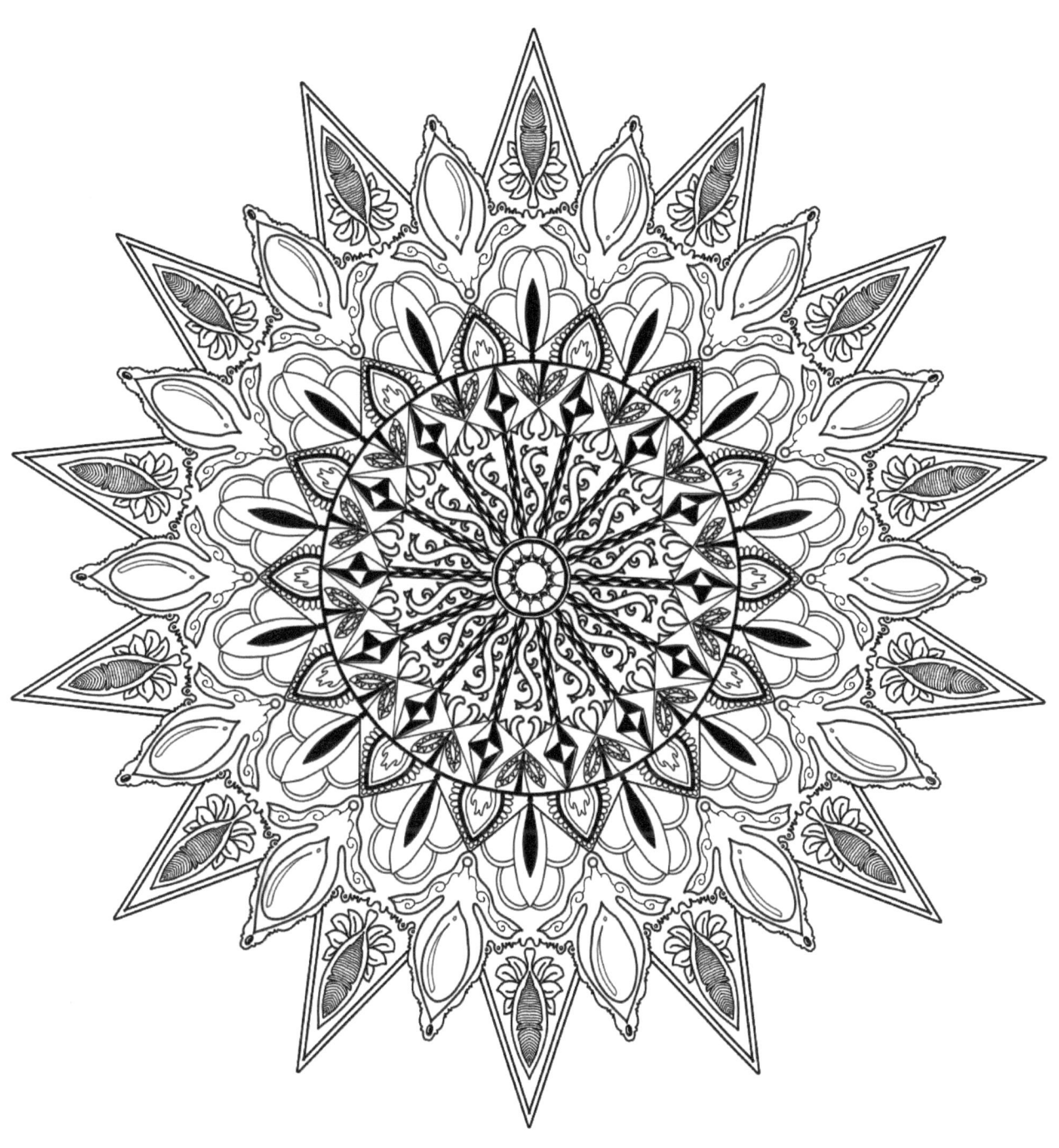

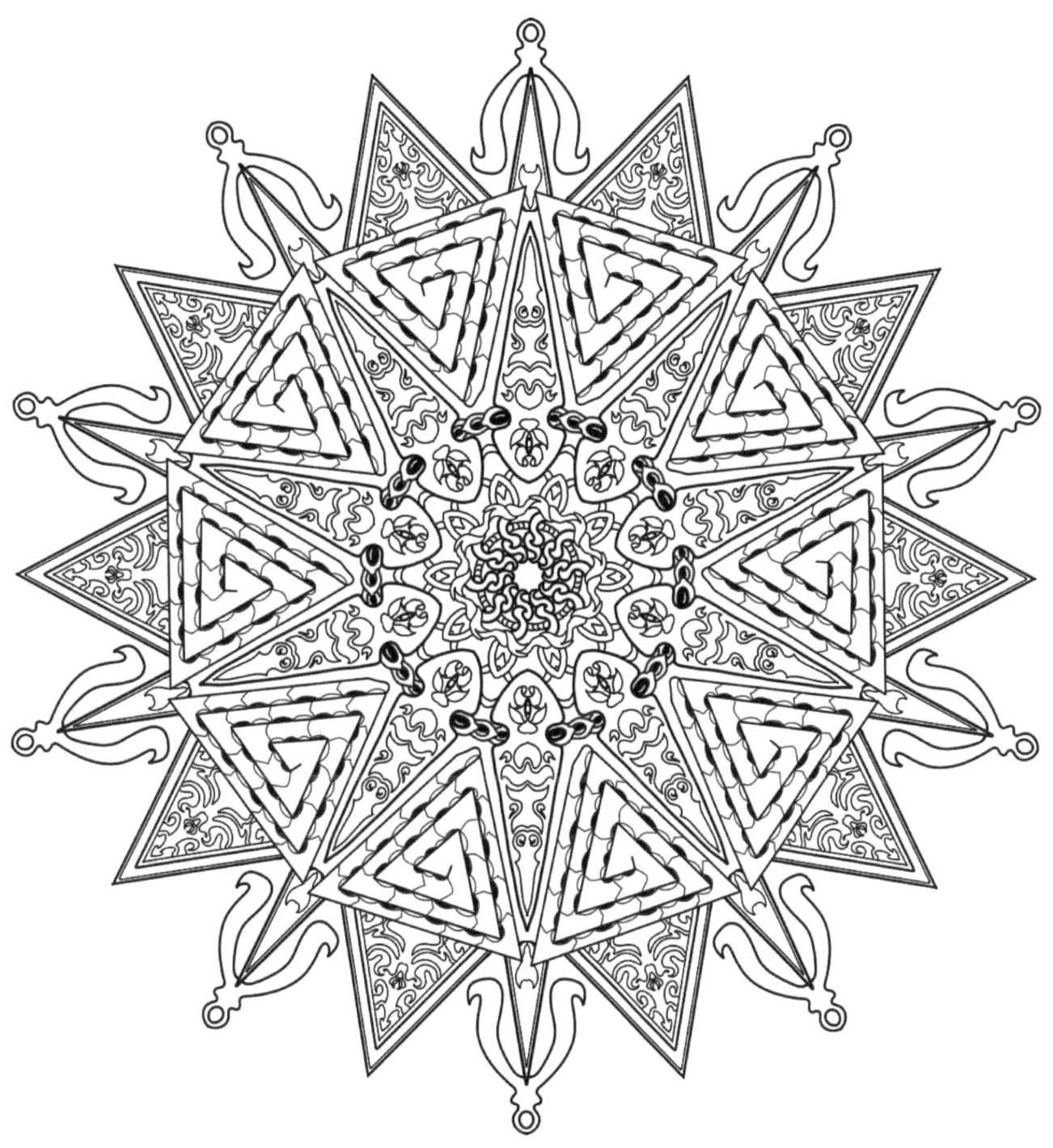

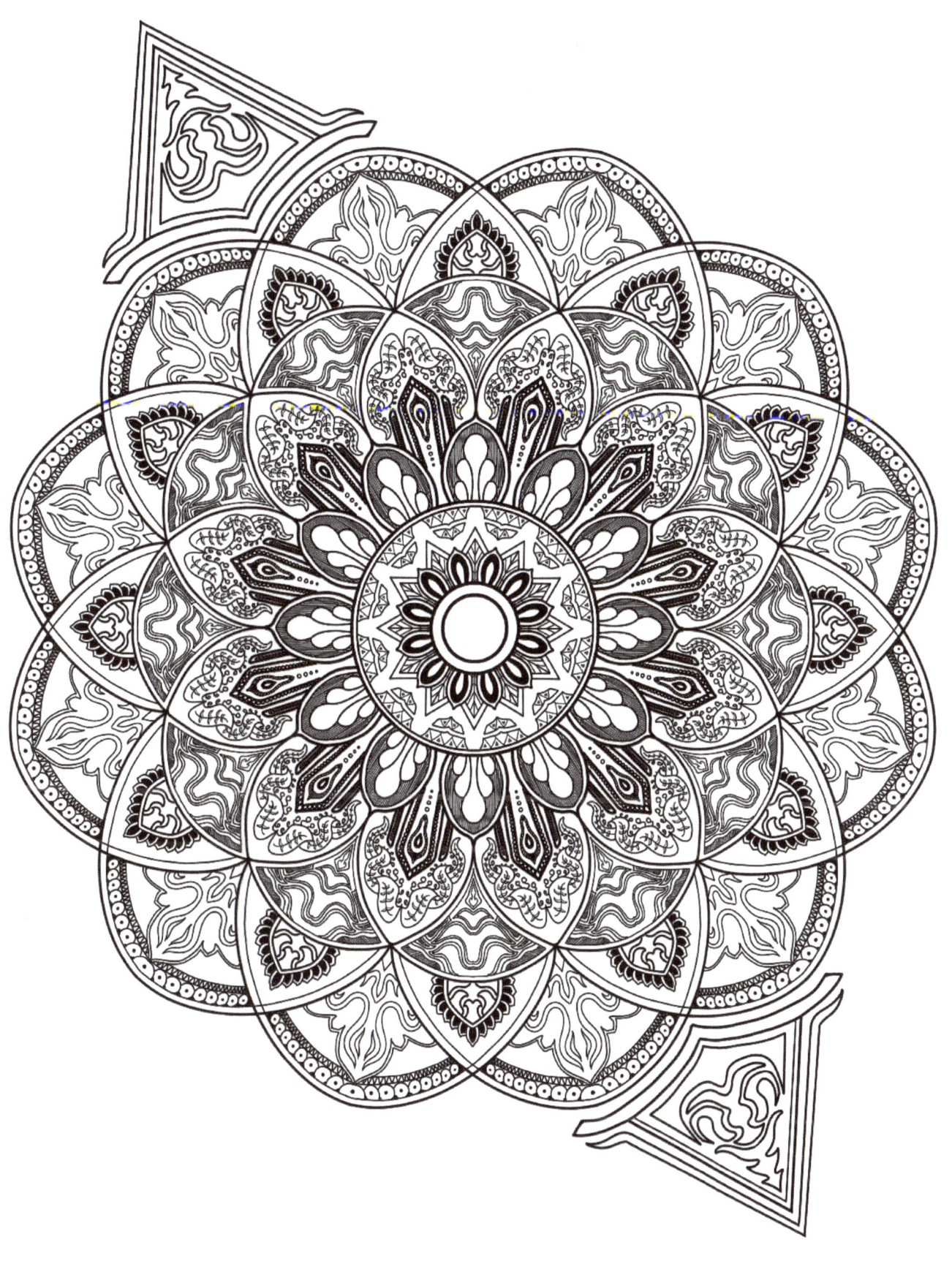

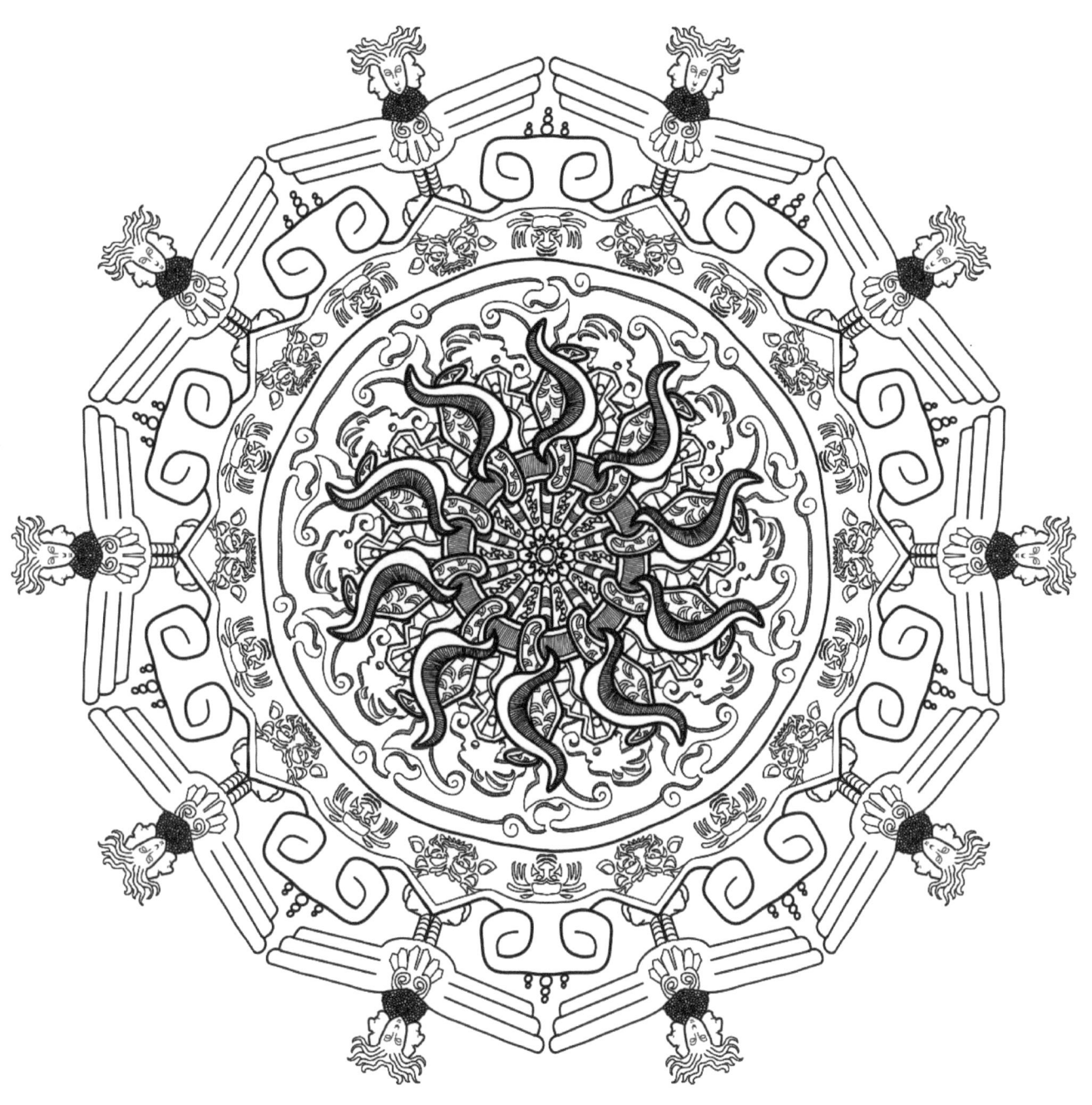

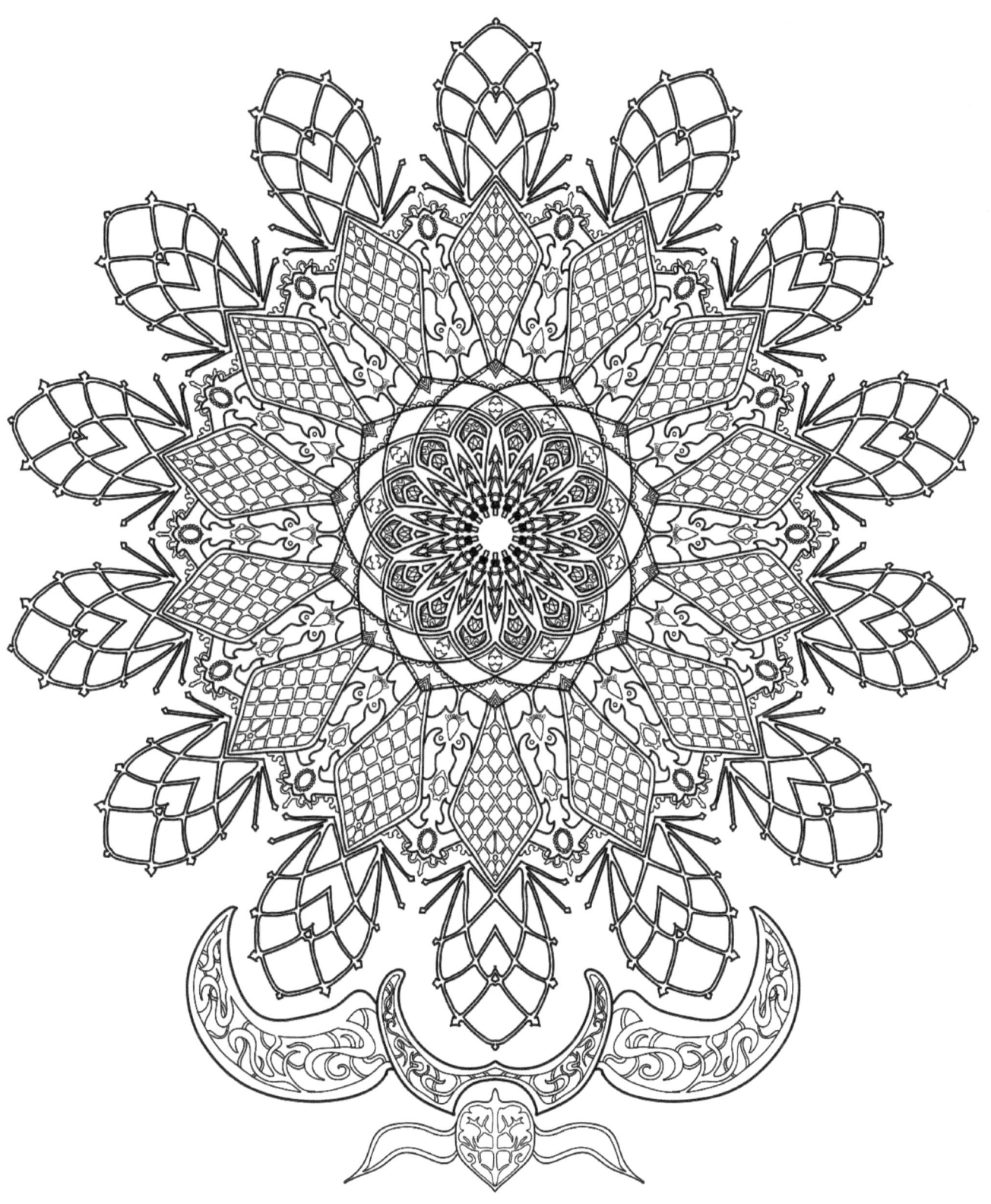

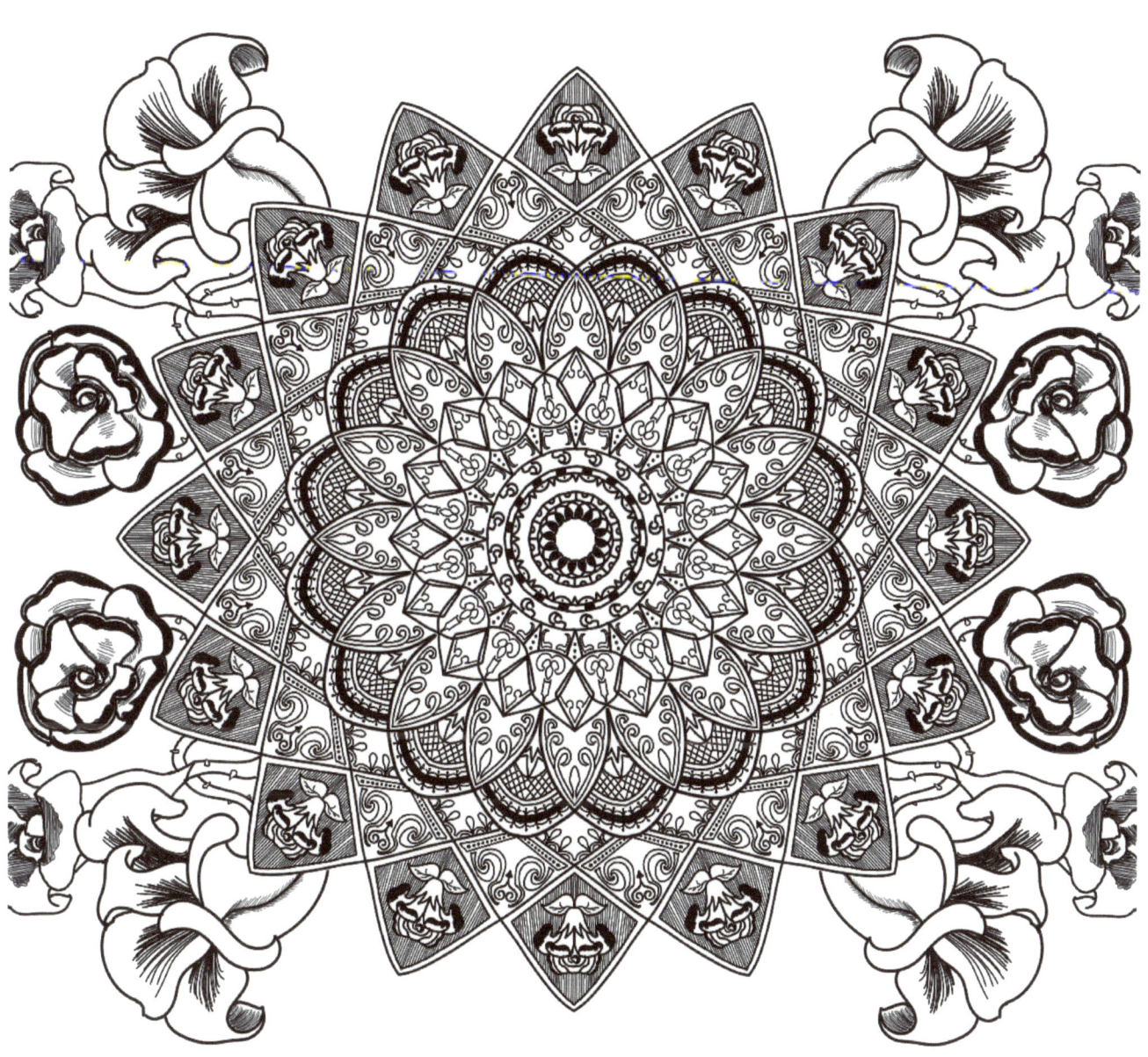

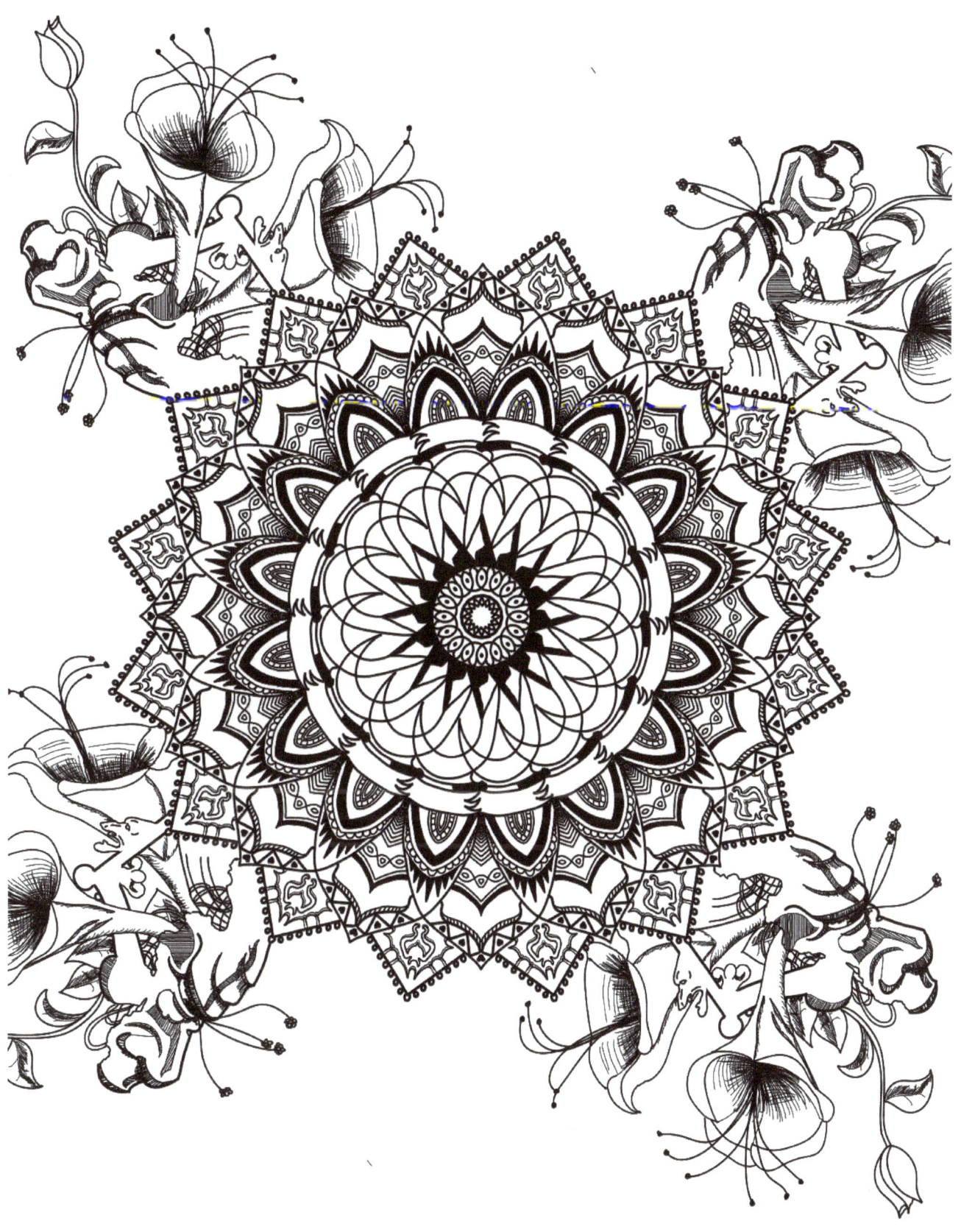

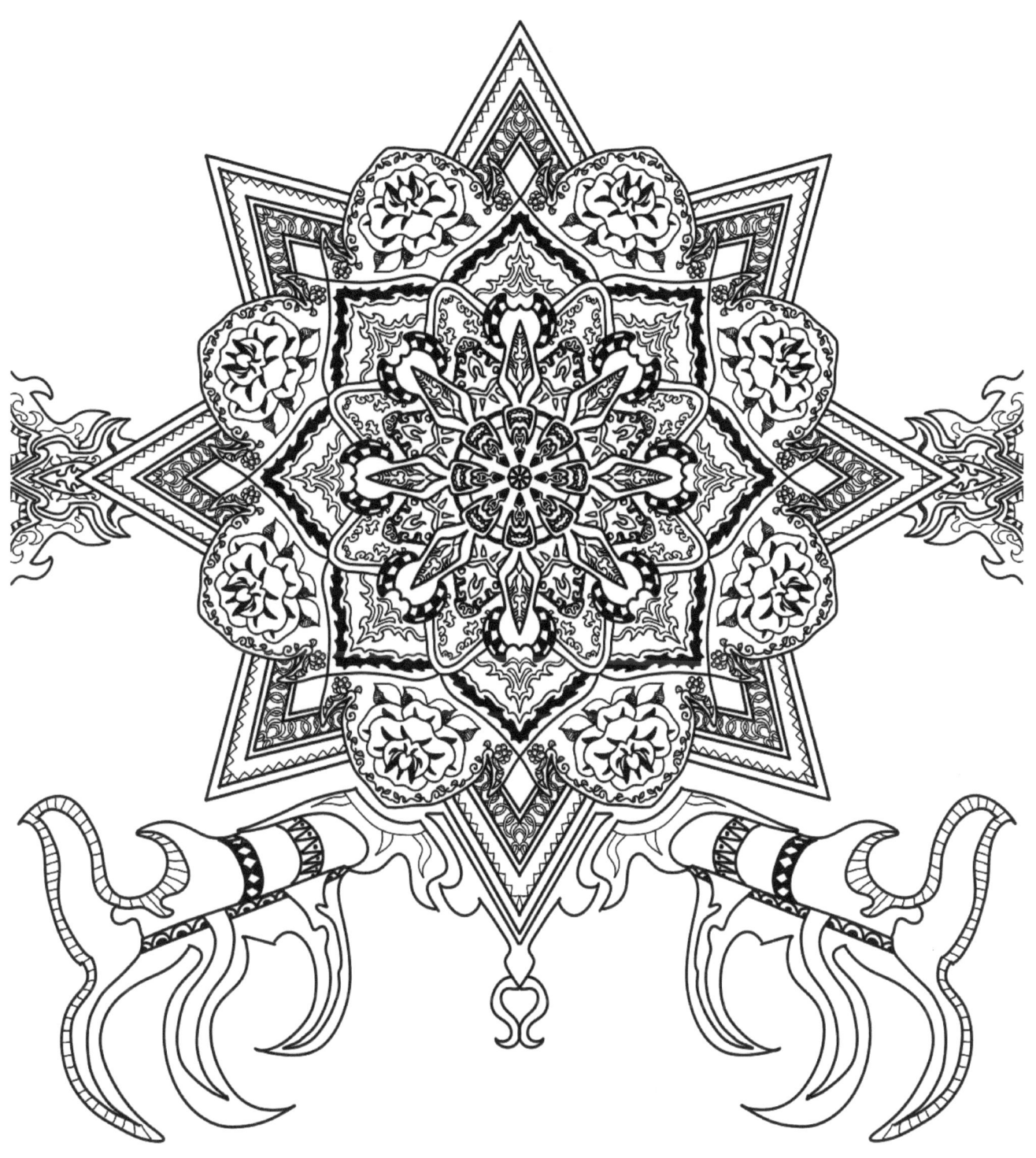

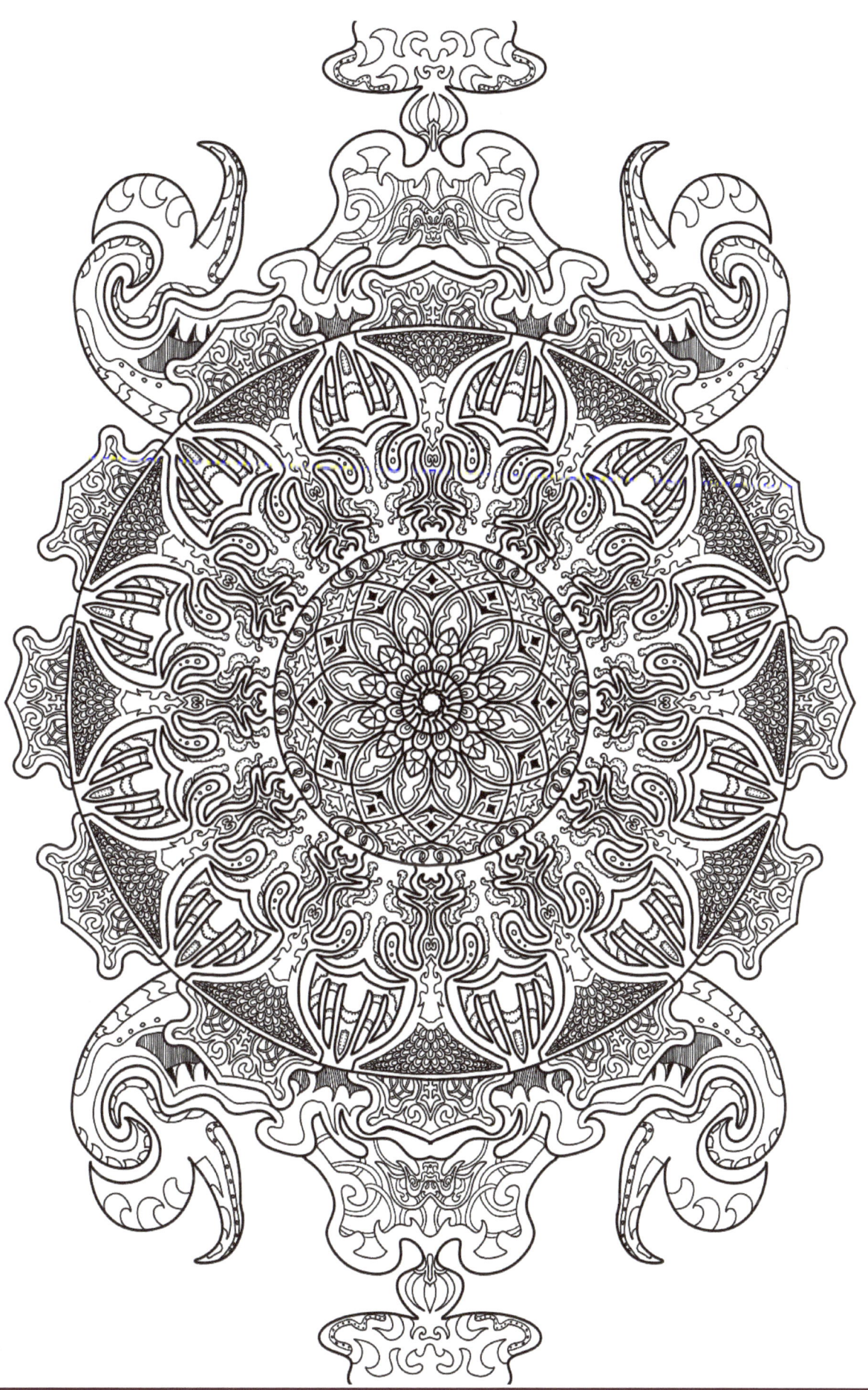

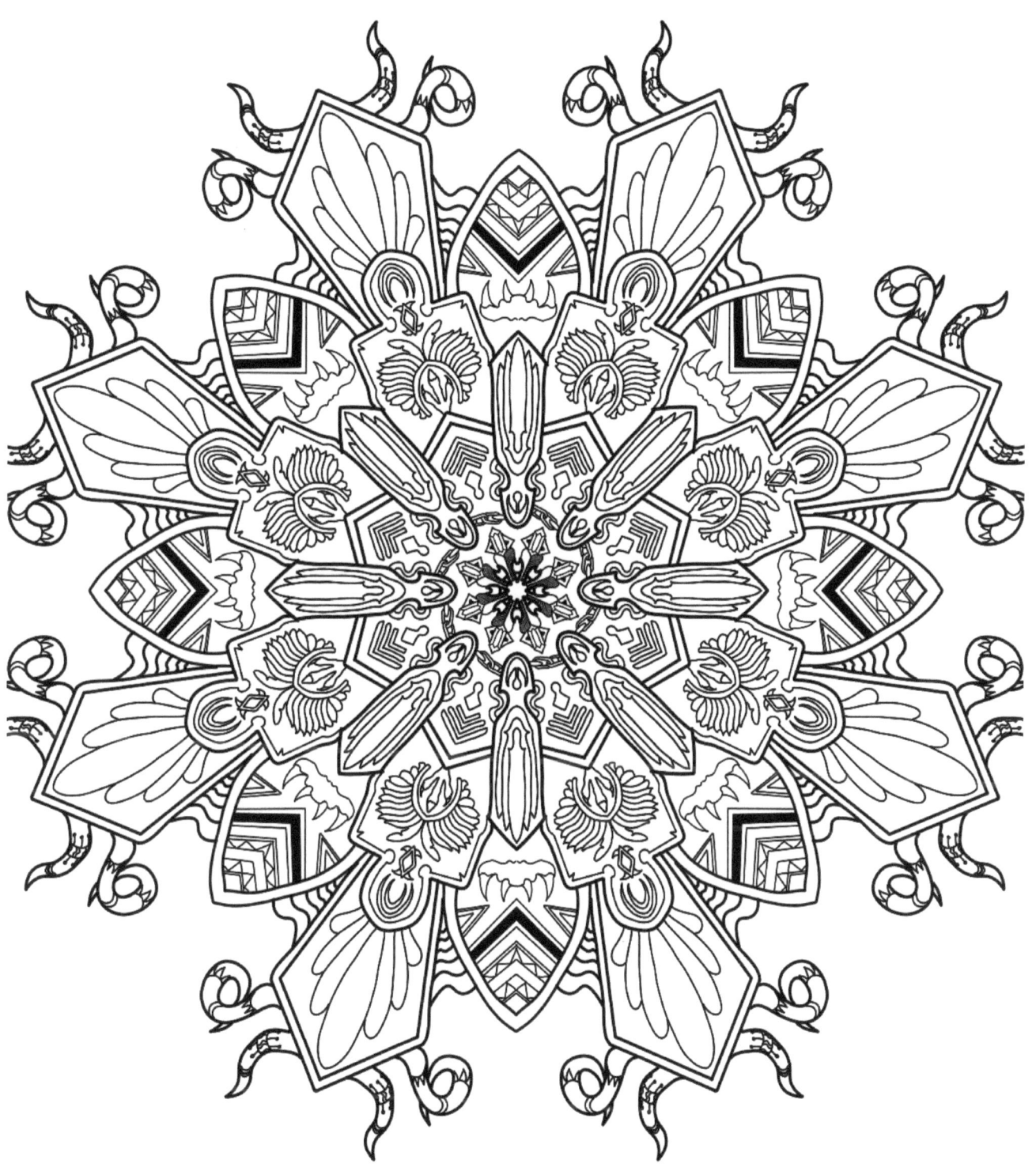

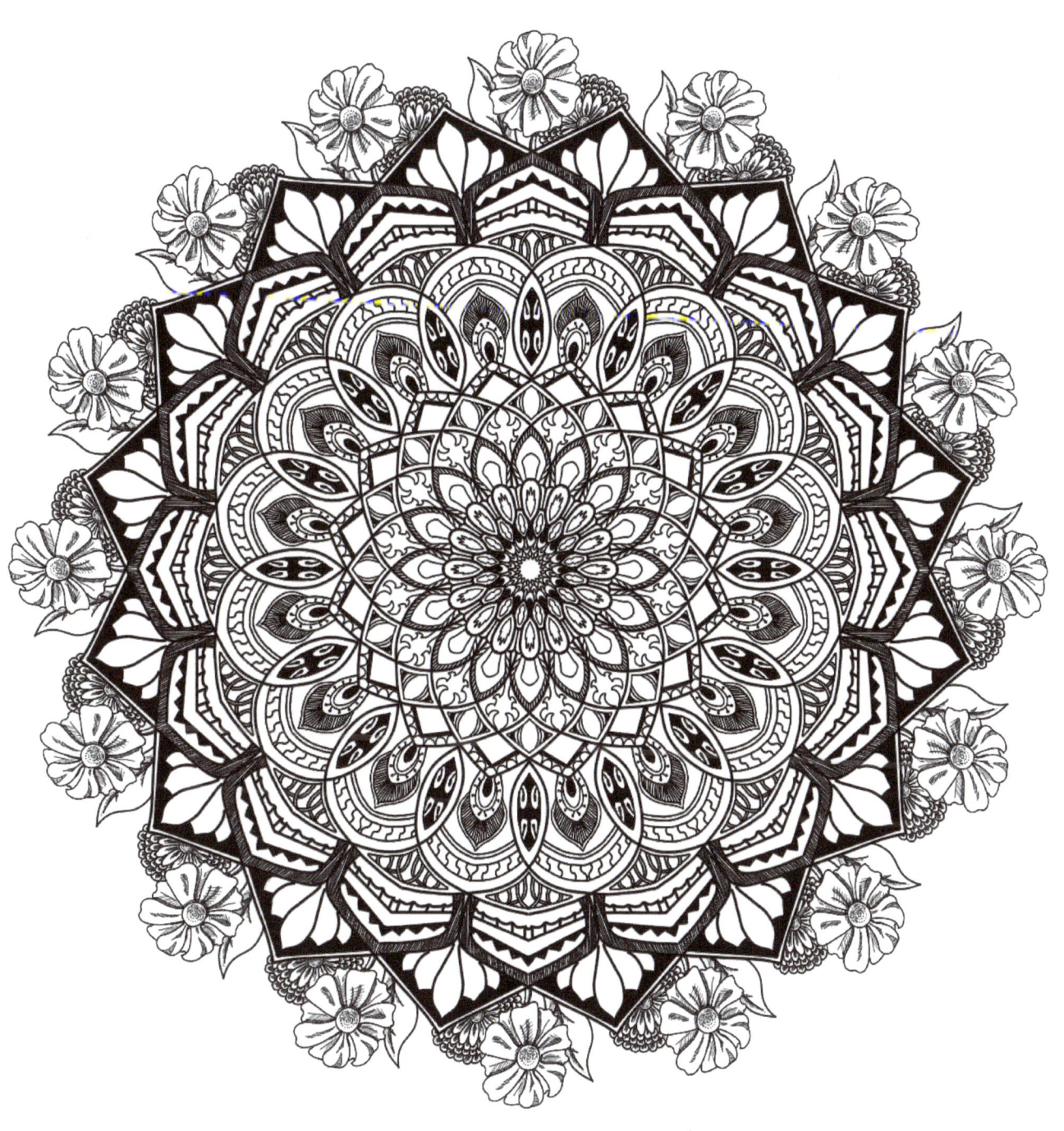

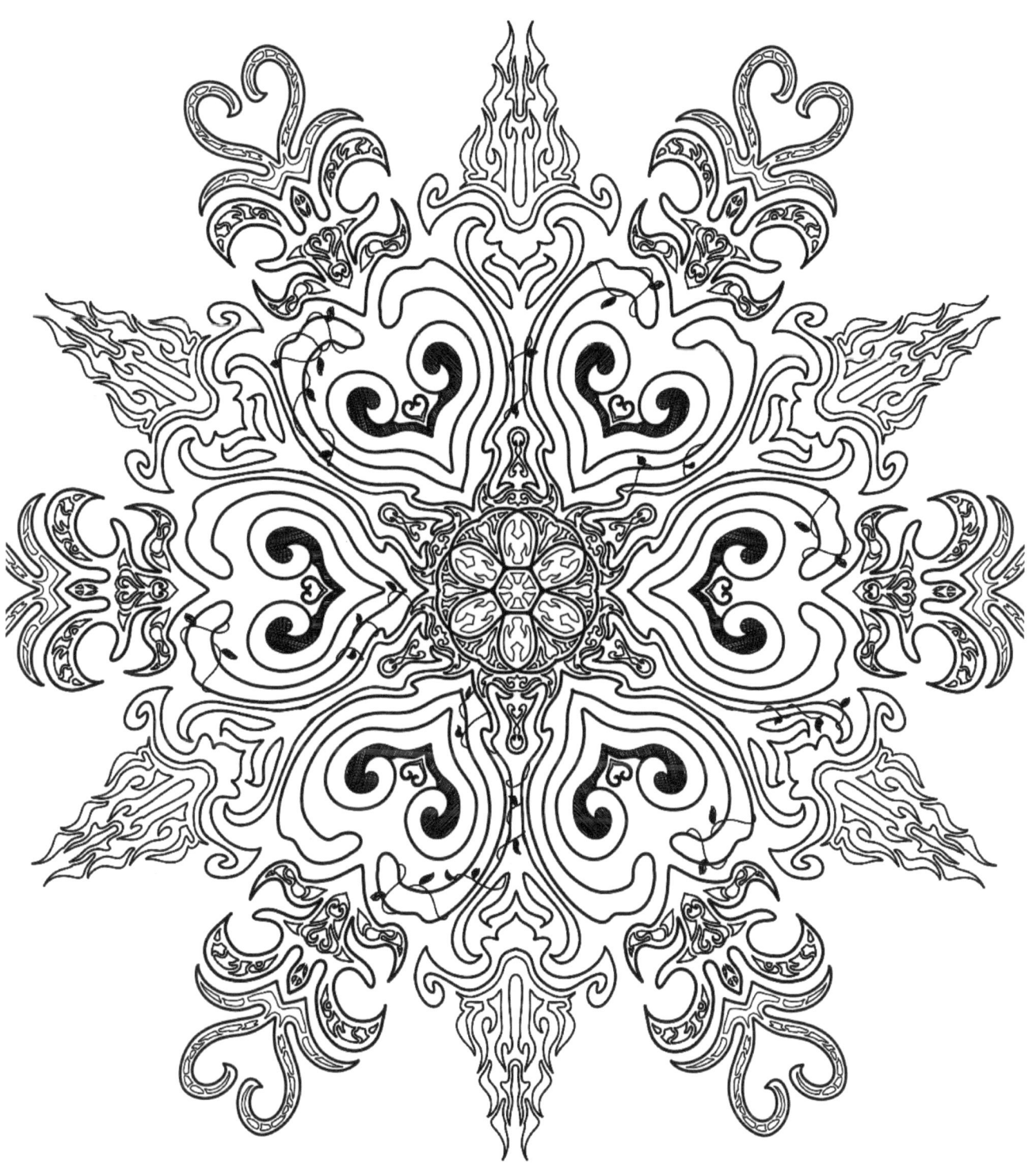

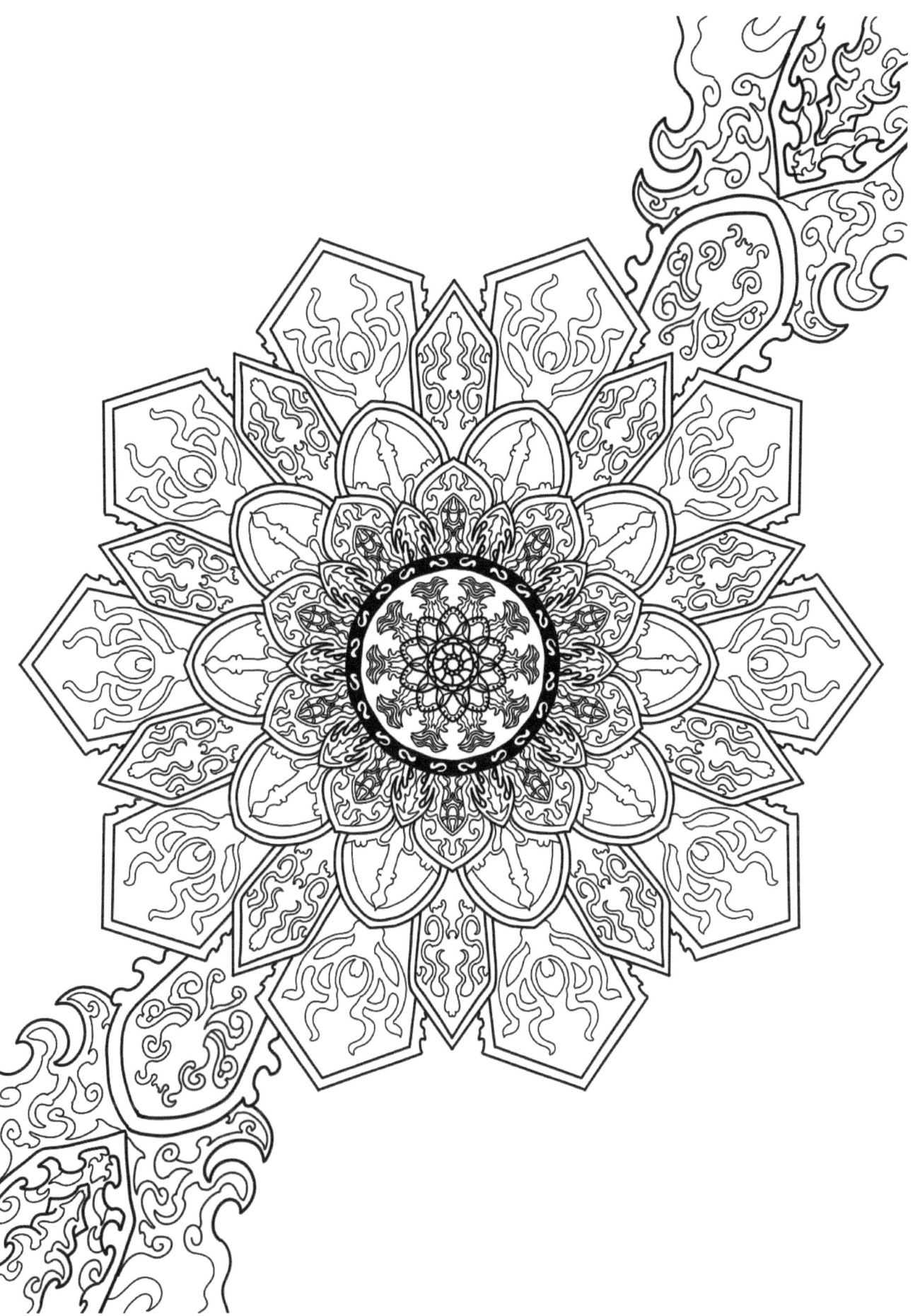

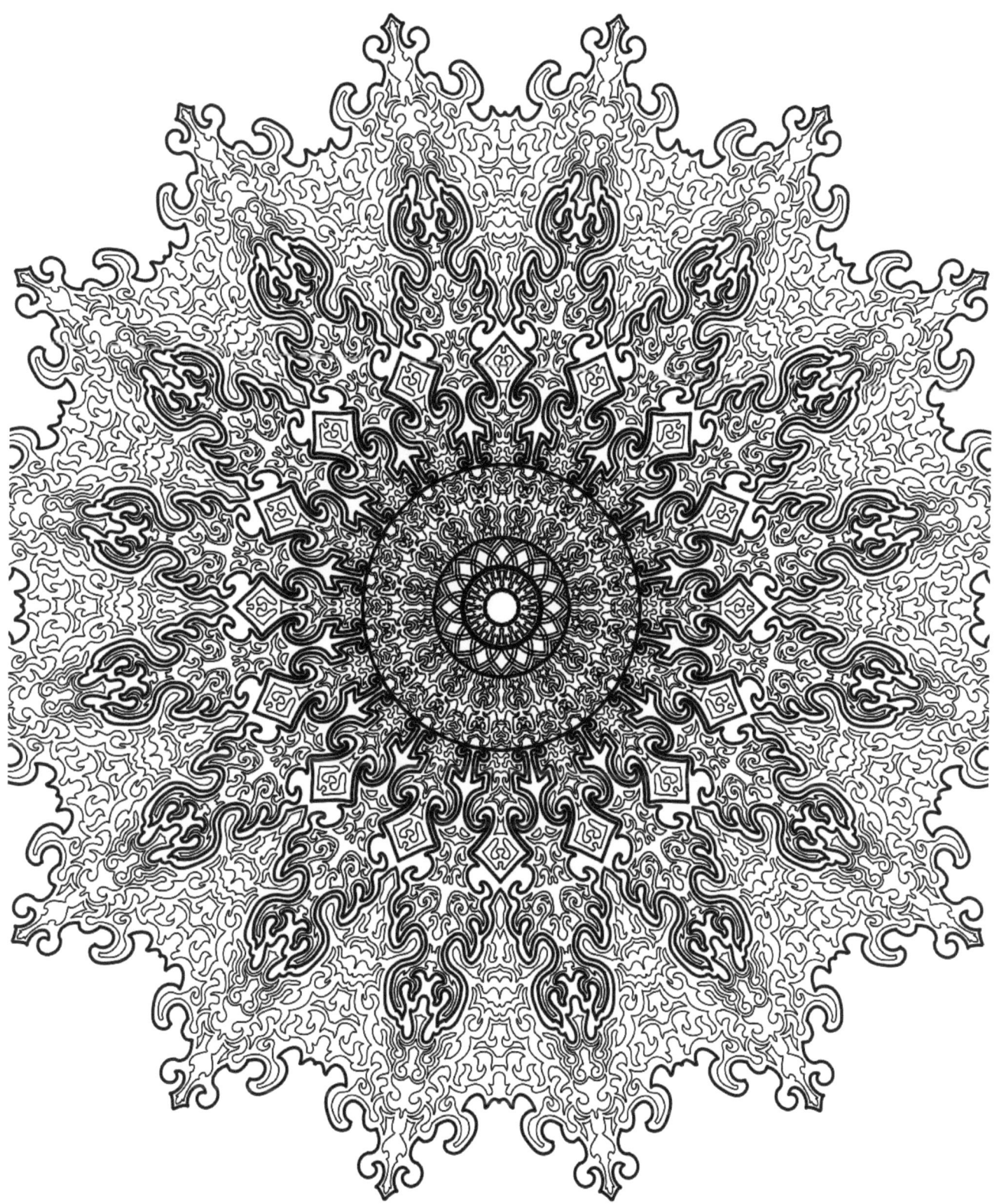

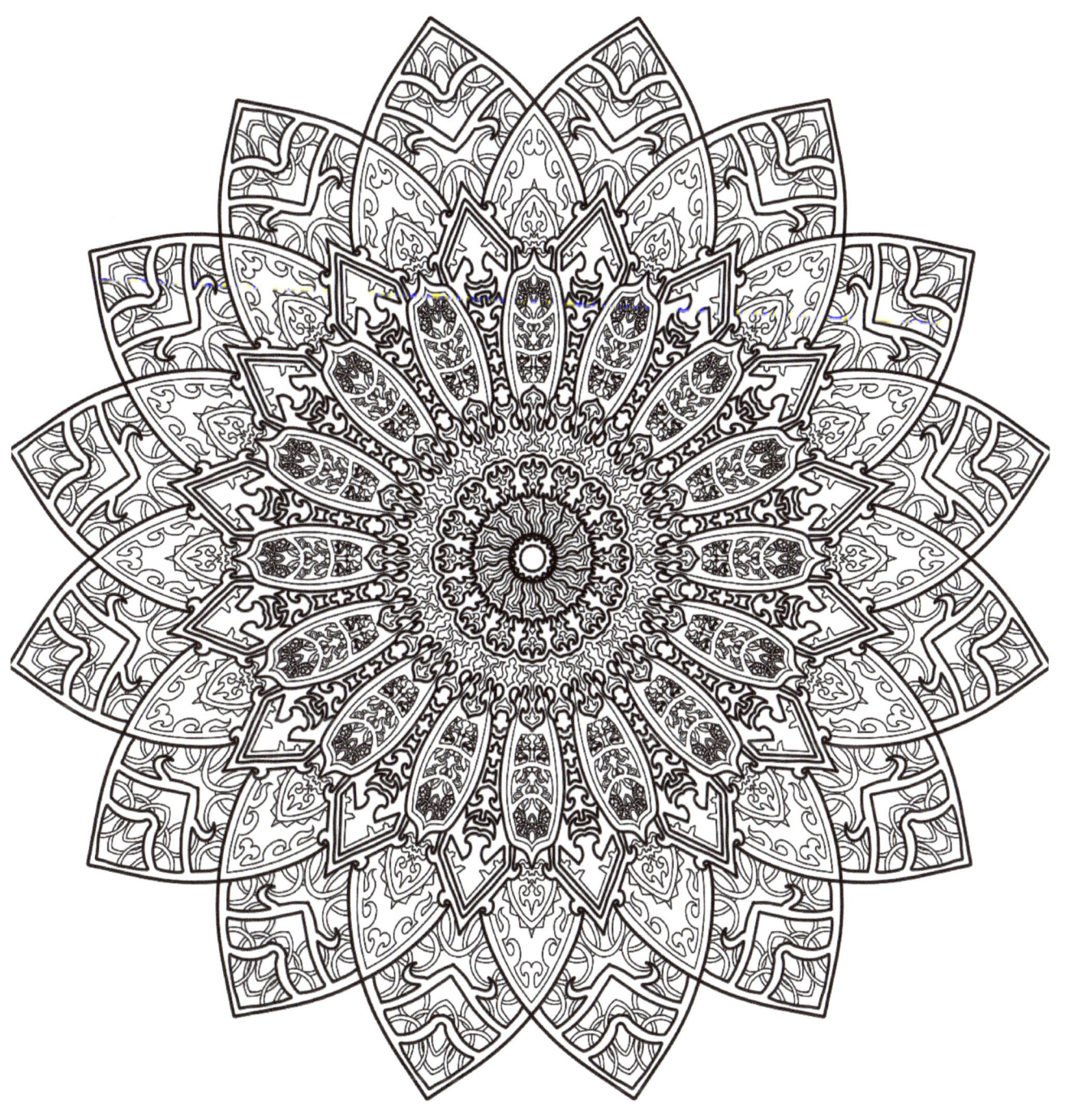

Check out some of the other JD-Biz Publishing books
[Gardening Series on Amazon](#)

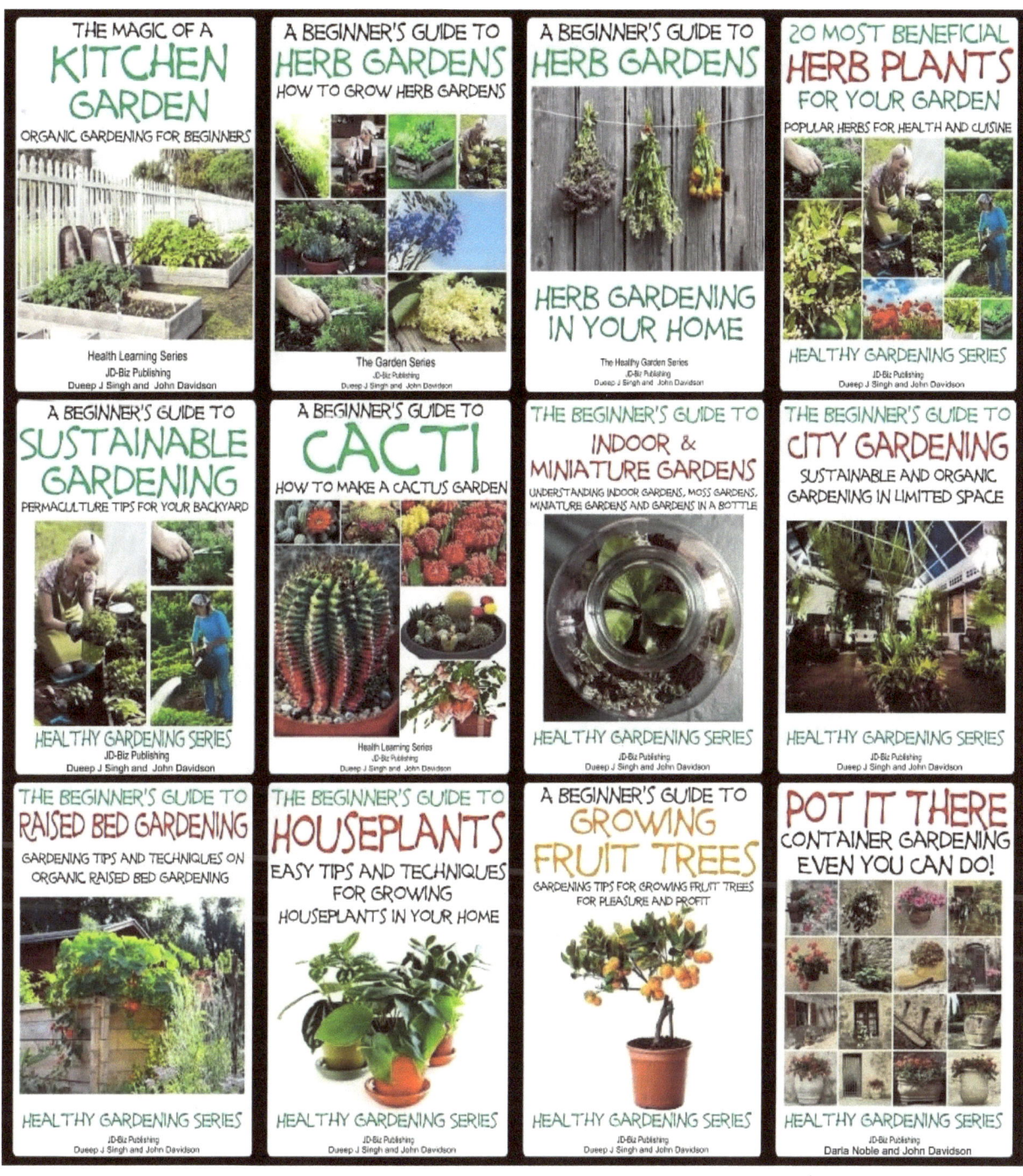

Download Free Books!
http://MendonCottageBooks.com

[Health Learning Series](#)

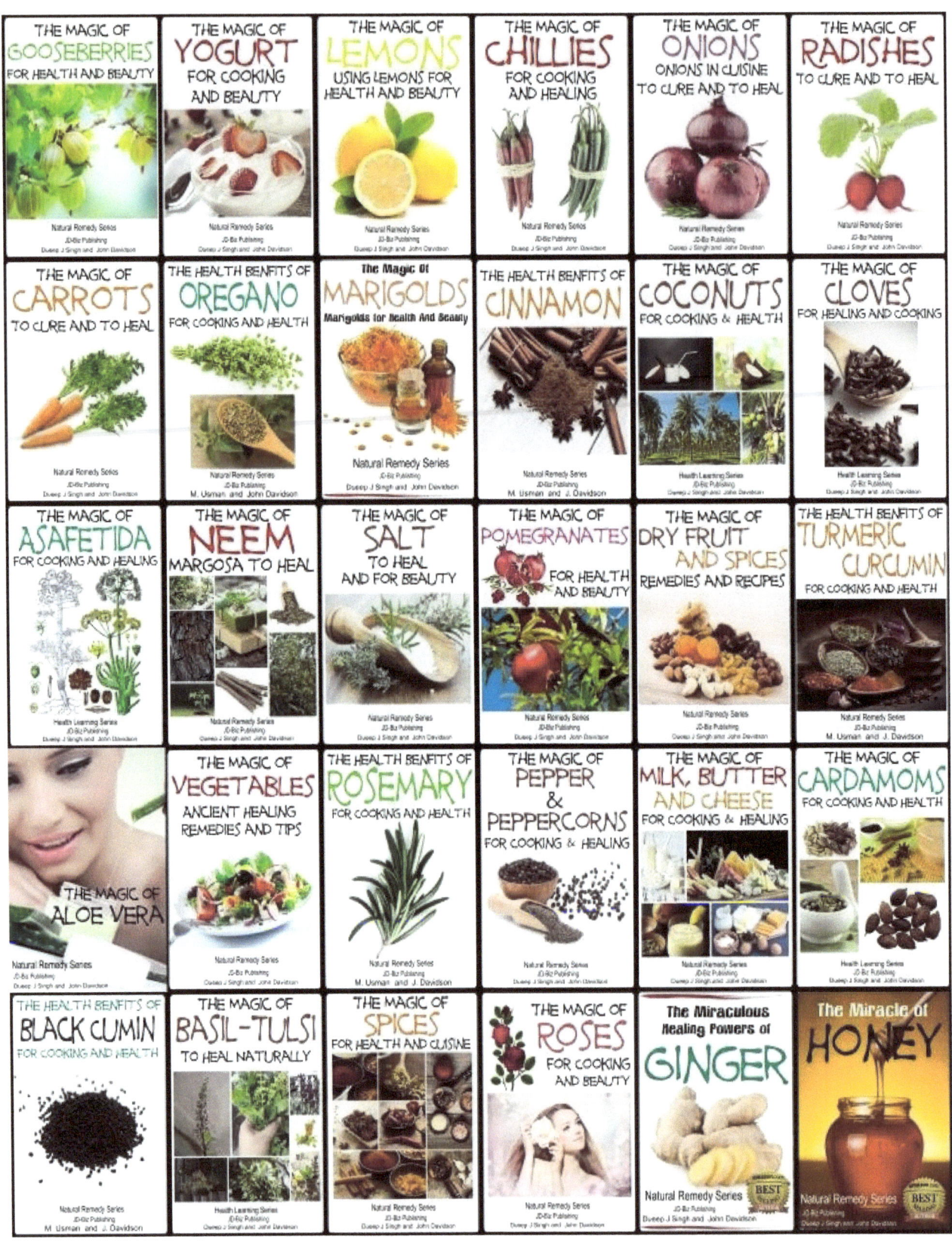

Country Life Books

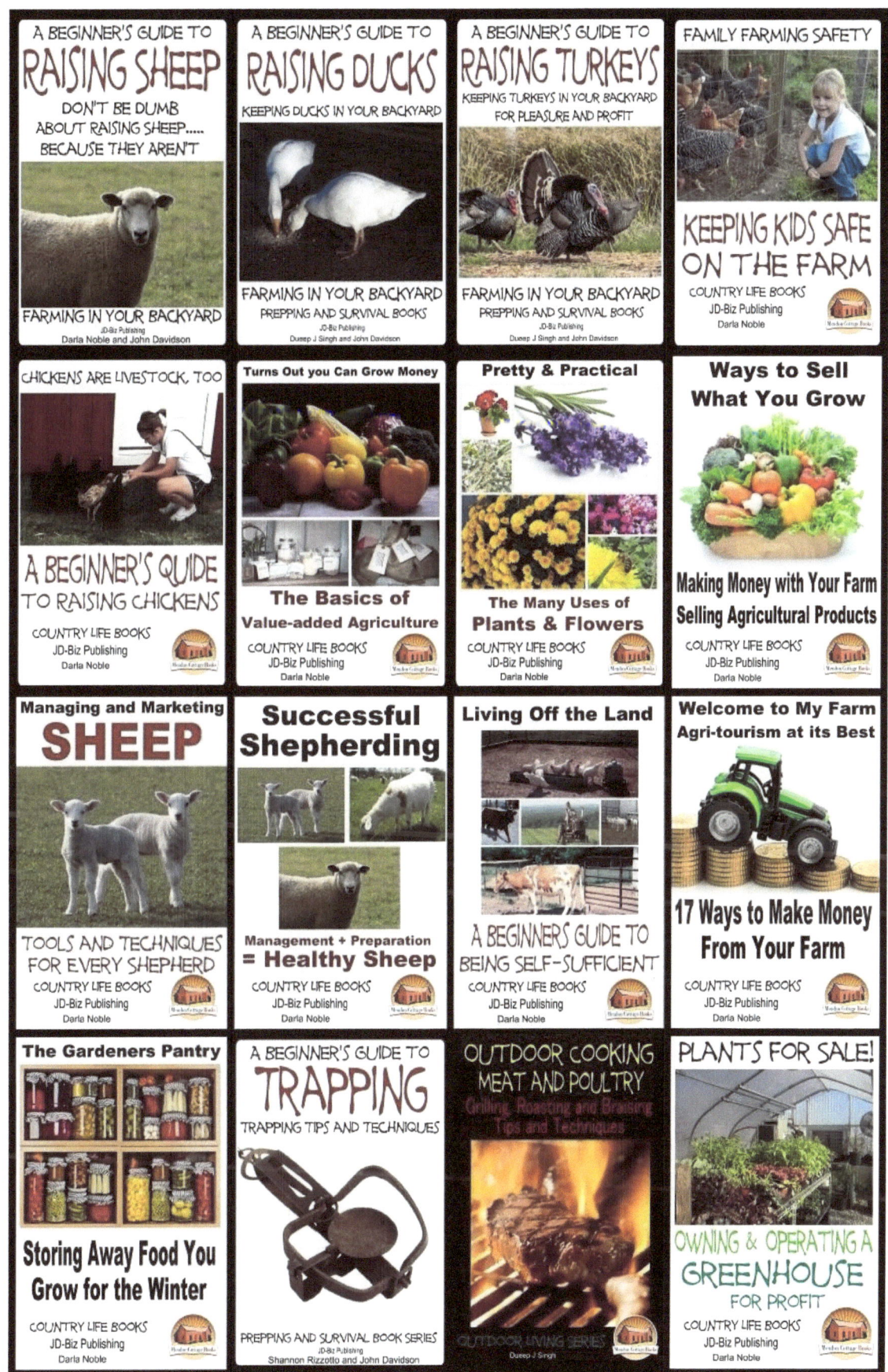

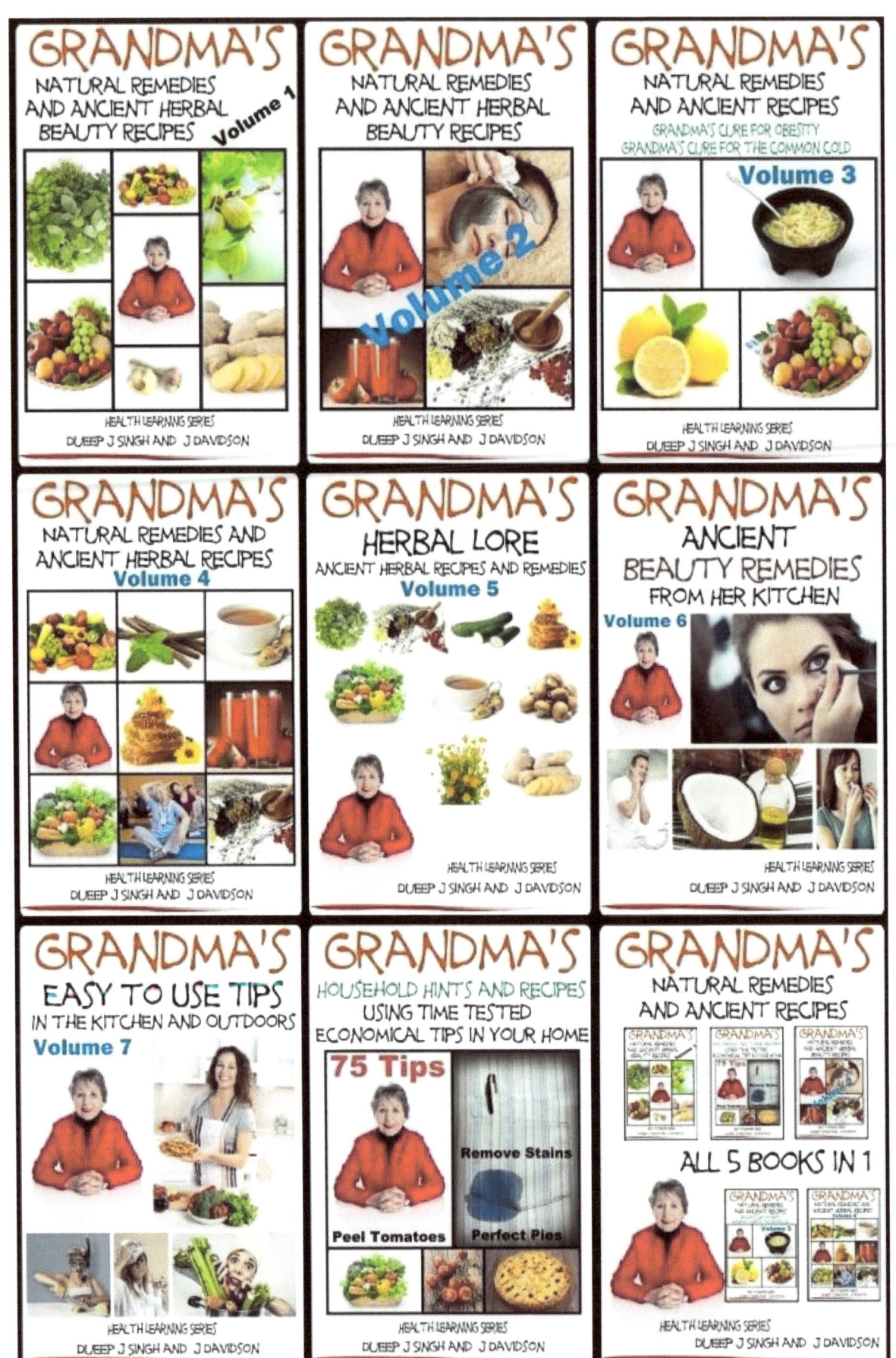

[Health Learning Series](#)

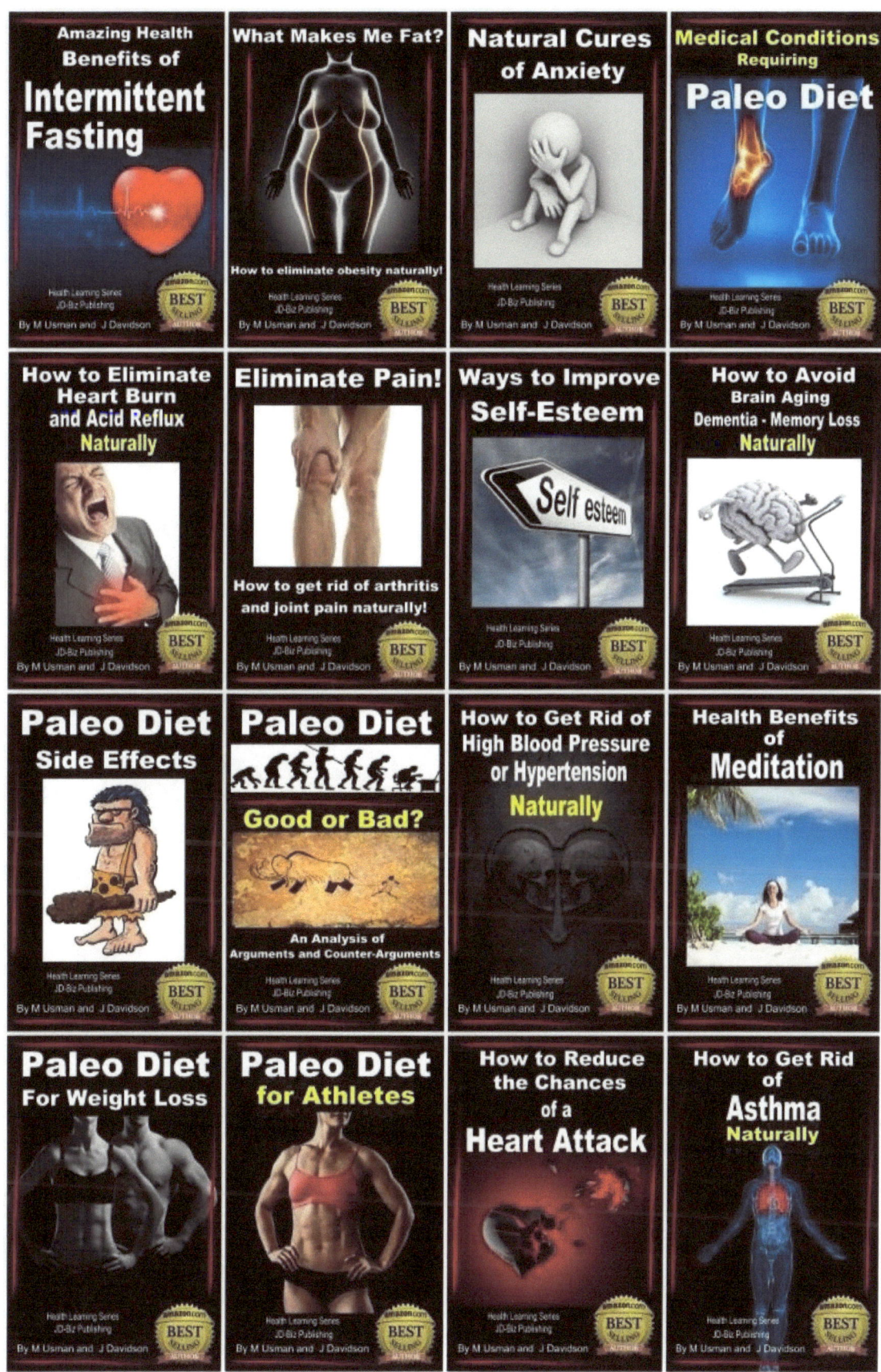

[Amazing Animal Book Series](#)

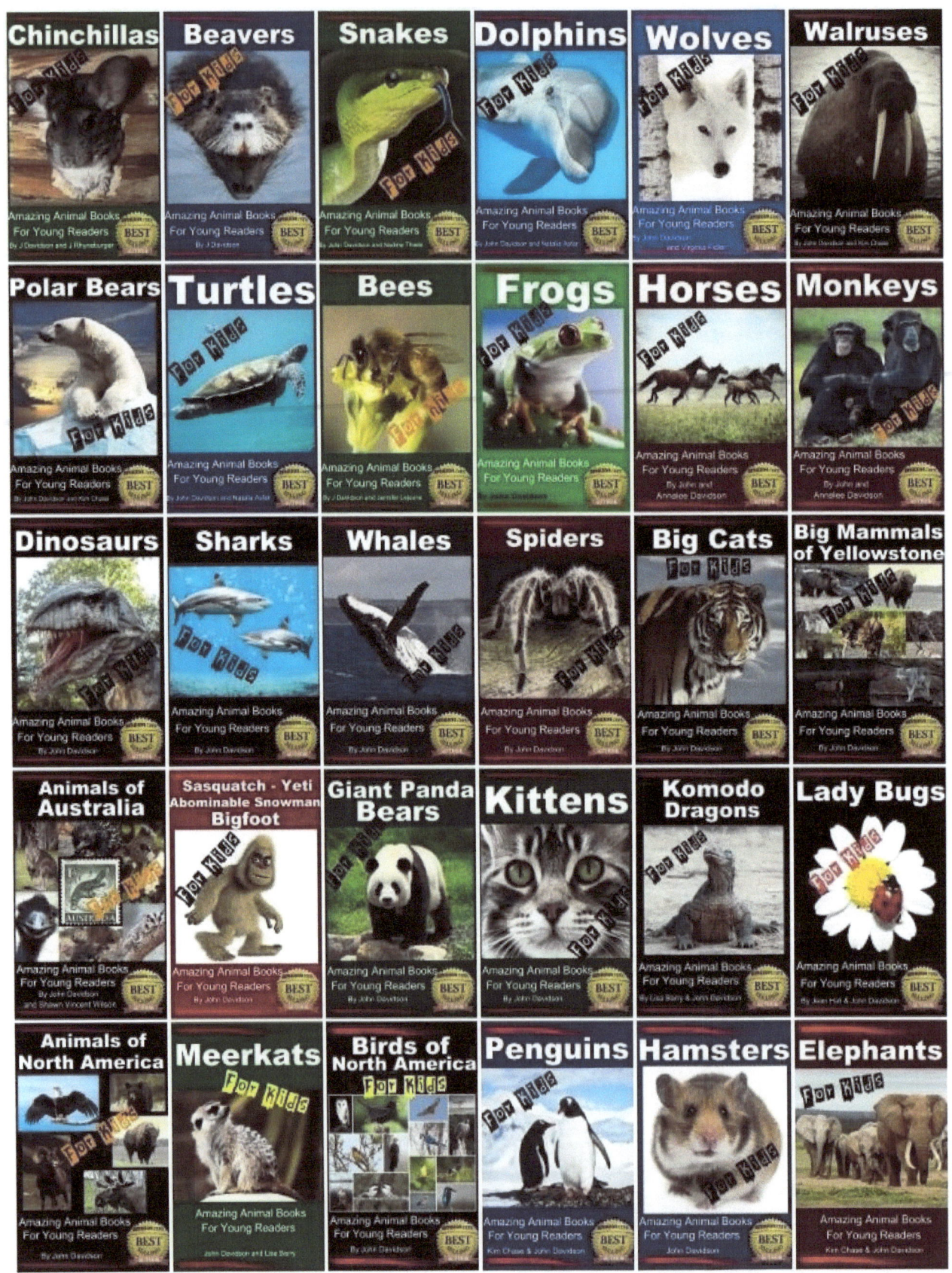

[Learn To Draw Series](#)

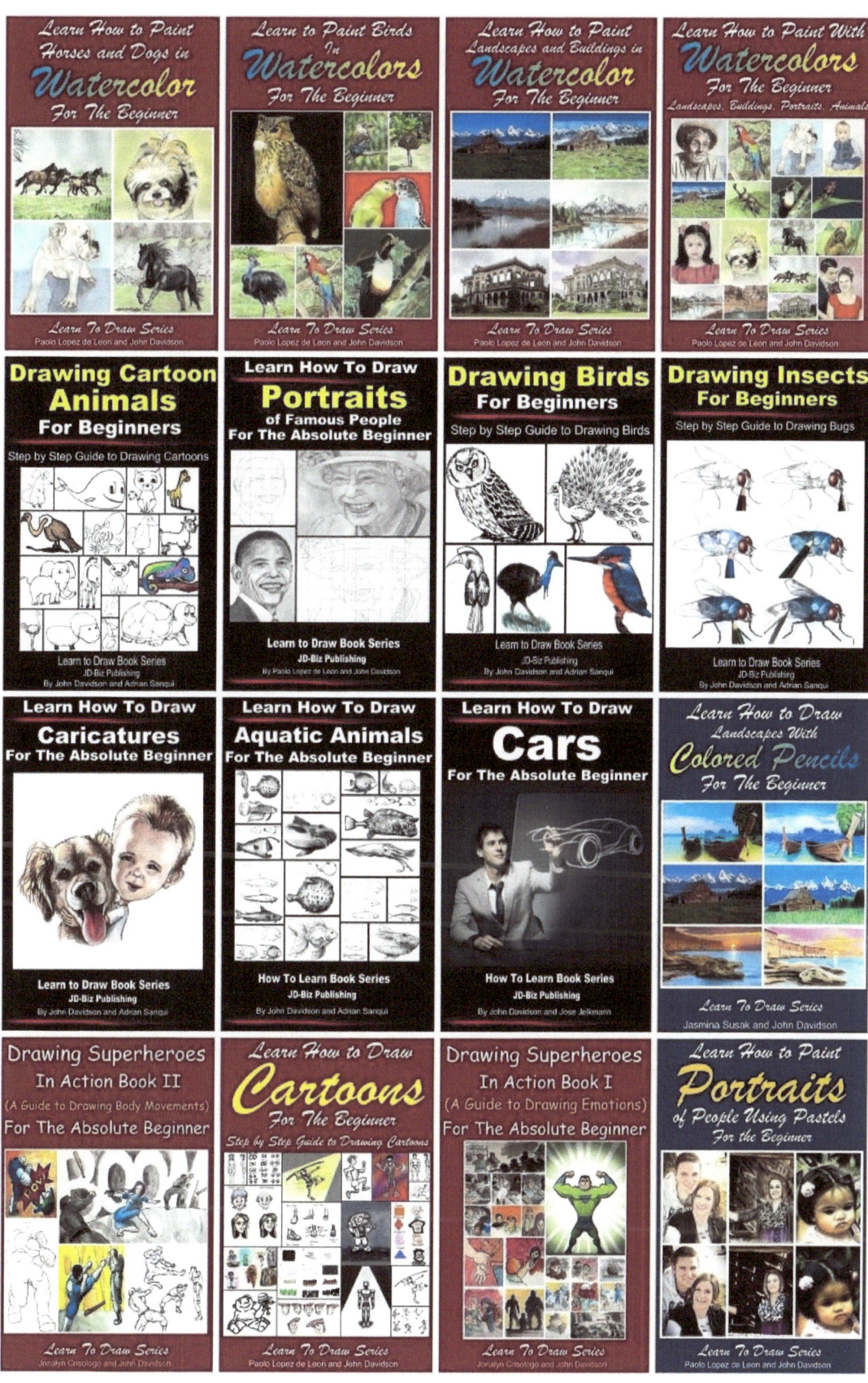

[How to Build and Plan Books](#)

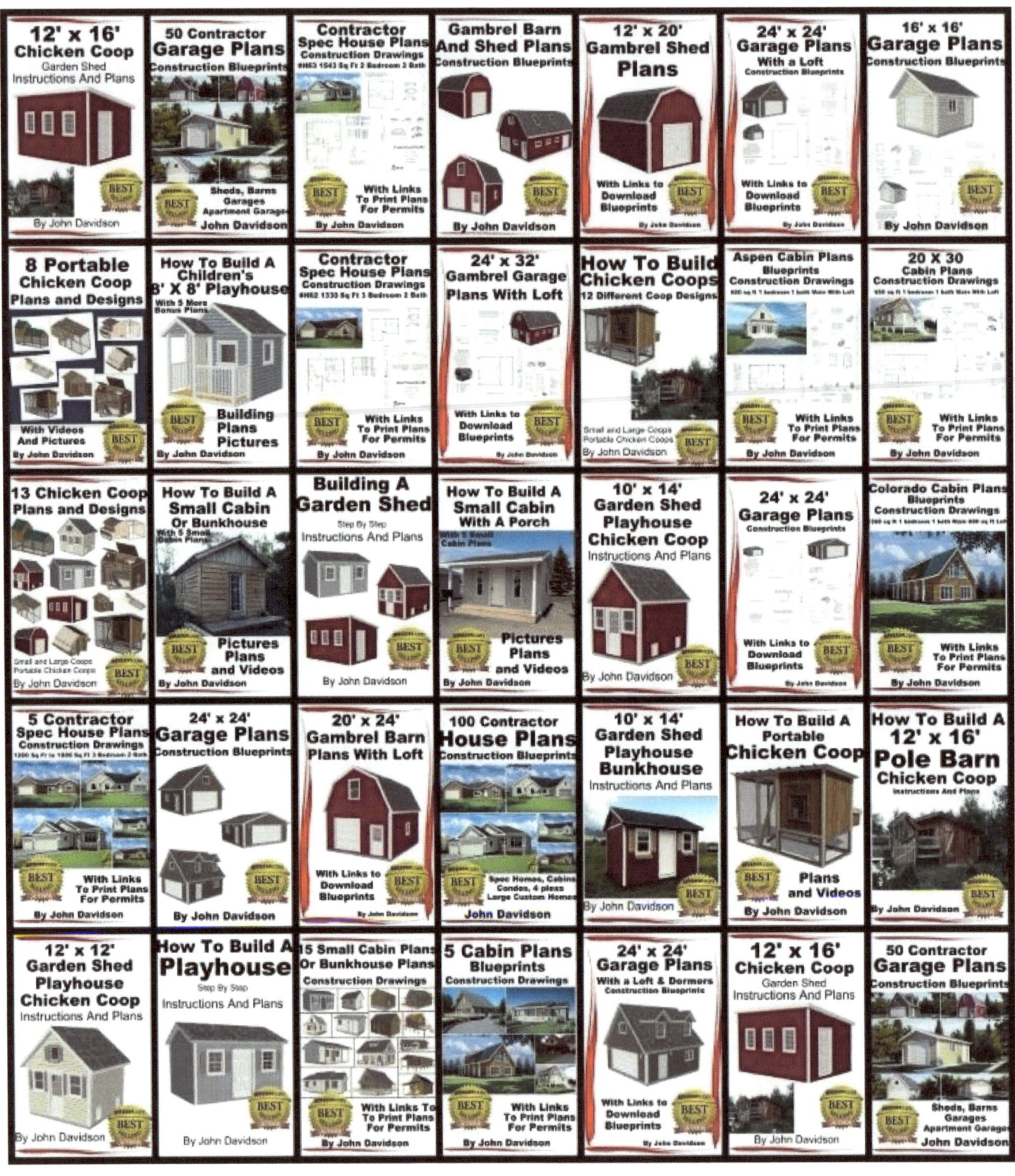

Entrepreneur Book Series

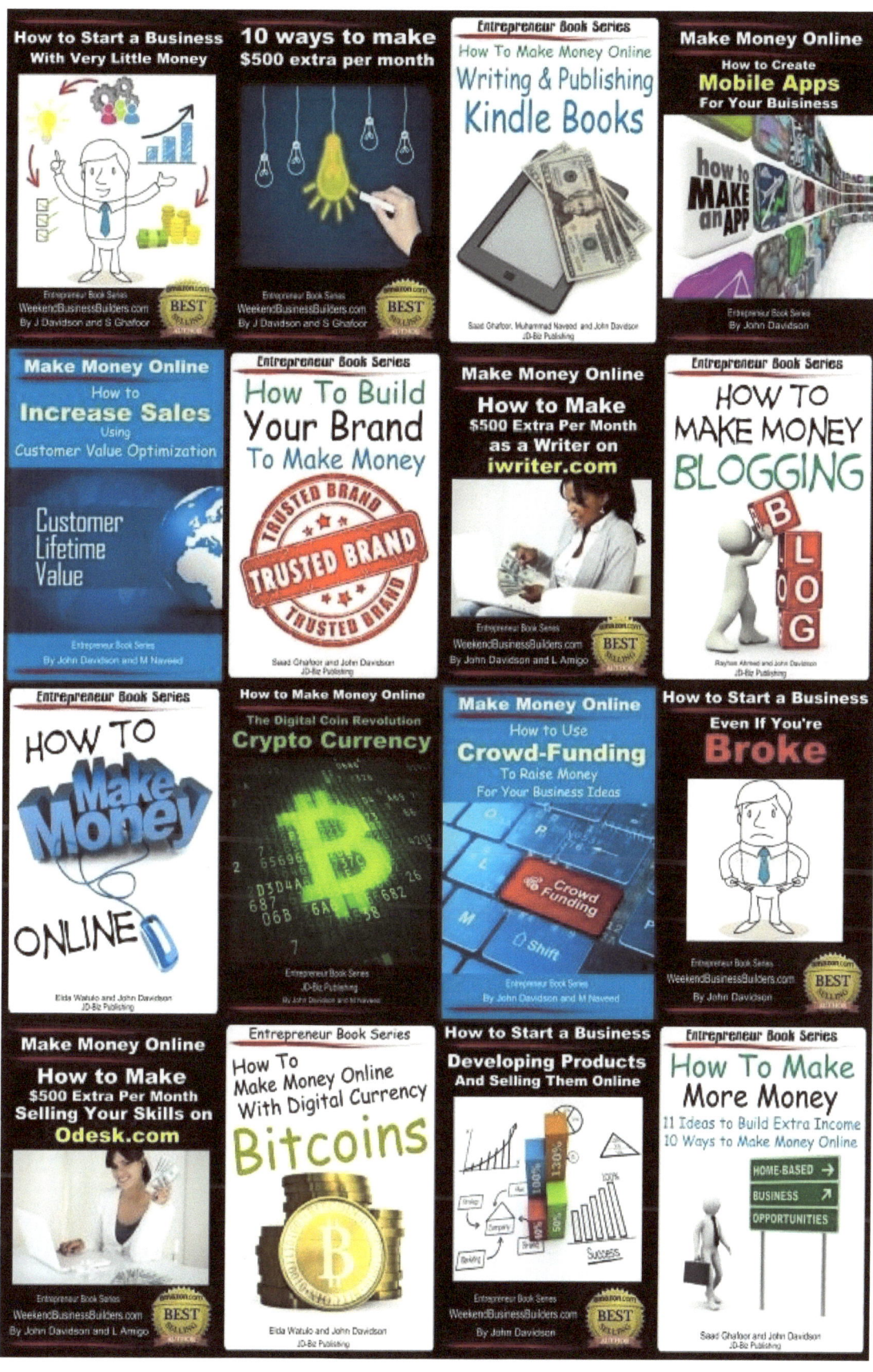

Our books are available at

1. Amazon.com
2. Barnes and Noble
3. Itunes
4. Kobo
5. Smashwords
6. Google Play Books

Download Free Books!
http://MendonCottageBooks.com

Publisher

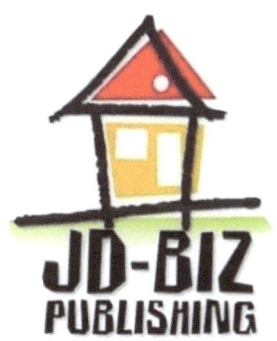

JD-Biz Corp

P O Box 374

Mendon, Utah 84325

http://www.jd-biz.com/

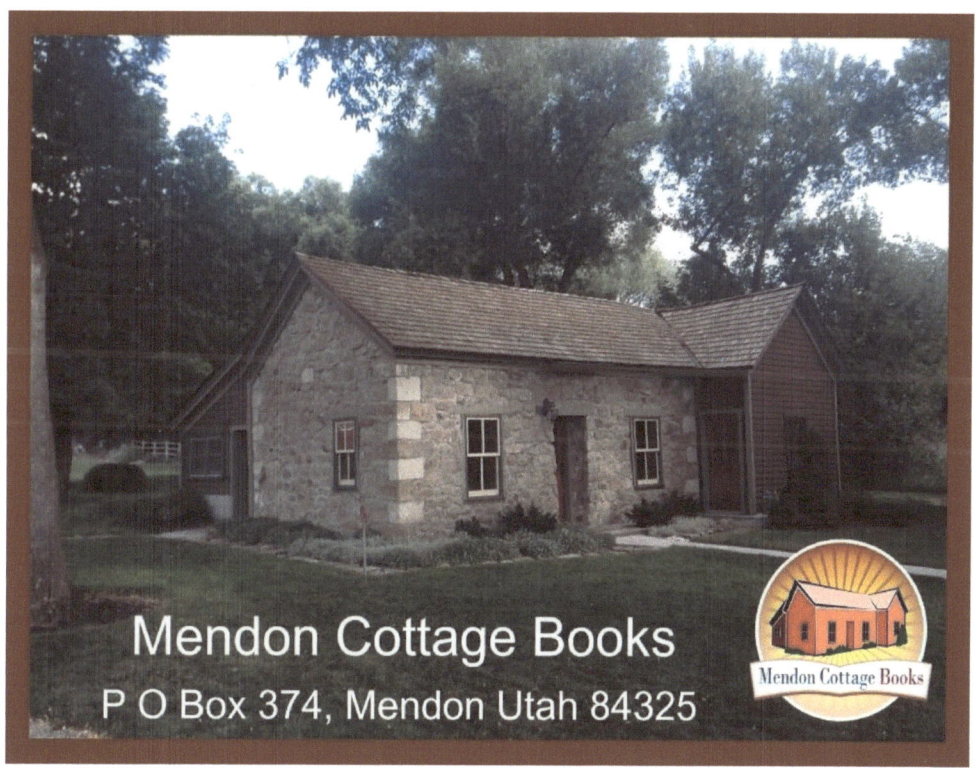

www.ingramcontent.com/pod-product-compliance
Lightning Source LLC
Chambersburg PA
CBHW051208220526
45473CB00003B/953